T0278724

SECRET
BUDAPEST

Géza Papp

JONGLEZ PUBLISHING

Travel guides

We immensely enjoyed writing the *Secret Budapest* guide and hope that, like us, you will continue to discover the unusual, secret and lesser-known facets of this city.

Accompanying the description of some sites, you will find historical information and anecdotes that will help you understand the city in all its complexity.

Secret Budapest also sheds light on the numerous yet overlooked details of places we pass by every day. These details are an invitation to pay more attention to the urban landscape and, more generally, to regard our city with the same curiosity and attention we often feel when travelling.

Comments on this guide and its contents, as well as information on sites not mentioned, are welcome and will help us to enrich future editions.

Don't hesitate to contact us:
Email: info@jonglezpublishing.com

THE AUTHOR

Géza Papp has been fascinated by Budapest since moving there in 1996. Reading about its history and architecture evolved into writing a blog about the city. His articles have been published on hg.hu, in Budapest Journal and in Octogon among others.

This book will not guide you to the main tourist attractions of the city of Budapest. Rather, it invites you to discover its secrets – the less often visited, but interesting places, whether a building, a statue or a park. It would like to draw attention to the multitude of details that you may have passed by already or maybe never heard of.

In the book, you will find references to events that enable visits to otherwise closed buildings and locations. Please find below a collection of them:

• Budapest 100: Organised by KÉK Contemporary Architecture Centre in the spring, it originally focused on 100-year-old buildings, but has recently shifted to being organised around one theme, such as the ringroad Nagykörút or the Bauhaus.
budapest100.hu/en/ and *kek.org.hu/en*
• Night of Museums: The night when museums and exhibition places open for the night and welcome visitors with special events, including guided tours to show hidden parts of buildings. Held around the shortest night of the year (Midsummer Day in June). Pre-purchased tickets (armband) are necessary.
muzej.hu/en
• European Heritage Days: Visits to places of culture that are otherwise closed to visitors. Third weekend of September.
oroksegnapok.gov.hu
• Design Week: Organised around contemporary design, the event includes guided tours, studio visits and many other events. Held in October.
budapestdesignweek.hu

• Green Walk: Organised by Hungary Green Building Council (HuGBC), the event is focused on sustainable solutions in architecture, including guided tours to modern and historic buildings. Held in September.
hugbc.hu

• Hungarian Memorials Day: The event focuses on Hungarian historic buildings, with events and visits in many locations. Held in May.
nori.gov.hu

• Archives Picnic: Organised by the archives of Hungary and of Budapest, the event enables access to some of the otherwise closed sections of the archives, a glimpse at historic documents, etc. Held in June.
archivportal.hu

• World Art Nouveau Day: The event focuses on Art nouveau-style buildings and exhibitions, organised by the Museum of Applied Arts. Guided tours, exhibition guides, worshops and film screenings are available. Held in June.
imm.hu

• Open Churches Day: Within the Ars Sacra festival, at the same time as the European Heritage Days, in September. Guided tours, organ concerts are organised.
ars-sacra.hu

• International Tourist Guide Day: Organised by the Budapest Chamber of Commerce and Industry, the day offers guided tours of Budapest in a variety of themes. Held in February.
bkik.hu

Another way to get into buildings that are otherwise closed to the public is to browse through the offers of guided tour organisers. They often organise visits to such places, but the offer is ever-changing. The best solution is to subcribe to their newsletters to follow up on the current offer. Please find below a short list:

- Hosszúlépés   *hosszulepes.org*
- Imagine Budapest   *imagine.hu*
- Budastep   *budastep.hu*
- Sétaműhely   *setamuhely.hu*
- Greetings from Budapest   *greetingsfrombudapest.hu*
- Korzózz velünk!   *korzozzvelunk.hu*
- Városművek   *varosmuvek.hu*
- Budai Várséták   *budaivarsetak.hu*

I hope you will find as much joy in discovering the hidden corners of Budapest as the author of this book.

Your feedback and suggestions to the author are most welcome at geza.papp.77@gmail.com and to the publisher at info@jonglezpublishing.com

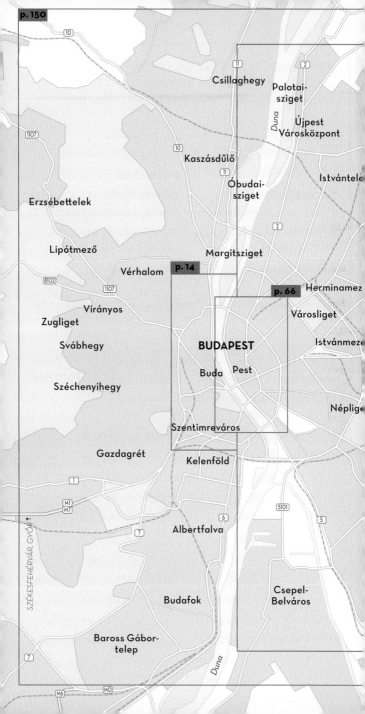

p. 216

Mogyoród

N

M3

M3

Rákospalota

M0

Pestújhely

Árpádföld

3

Alsórákos

M0

Kiszugló

3102

Sashalom

Törökőr

3

Mátyásföld

Ligettelek

31

Óhegy

31

4

Rákoshegy

M5

Kispest

Ferihegy

Budapest-
Ferenc Liszt

Szemeretelep

4

4601

M5

KECSKEMÉT, SZEGED

0   2   4 km

CONTENTS

Central Buda

Central Pest

Buda

CONTENTS

Pest

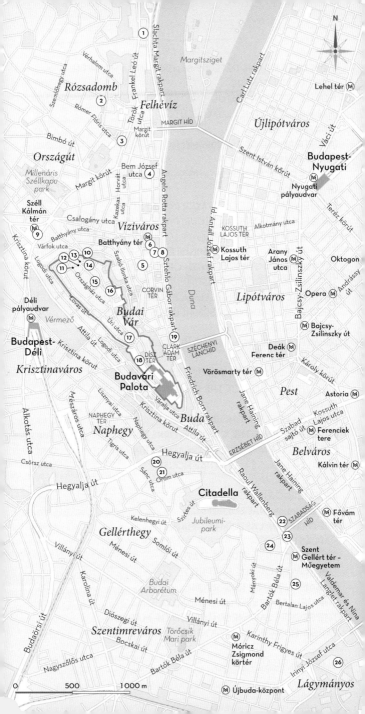

Central Buda

FRANKEL SYNAGOGUE

A synagogue hidden in the courtyard of an apartment house

1023 Budapest, 49 Frankel Leó út
Guided tours only, see introduction for operators
Tram: 17, 19, 41 – Komjádi Béla utca
Bus: 9, 109 – Császár-Komjádi uszoda

Surrounded on three sides by a six-storey apartment block, the Frankel Synagogue is easy to miss. The only decent view is of the rear façade from the Danube side and possibly through the main cast-iron gate at the front. Designed by Sándor Fellner, the synagogue opened at 8 o'clock on 8 August 1888 (8/8/1888) (see below regarding the symbolism of the number 8). The apartment block surrounding it (designed by Dezső Jakab and Aladár Soós) was built later, in 1928.

In comparison to the impressive Óbuda synagogue, built in 1769, the Frankel Synagogue is the result of the Tiszaeszlár Affair of 1882–83: False accusations against Jews accused of ritually murdering and beheading a girl sparked antisemitic agitation in Austria-Hungary, and encouraged the builders of the synagogue to build it as discreetly as possible.

Several famous people have attended the synagogue: Technical University Professor Ignác Pfeiffer; 1928 Amsterdam Olympic games champion Ferenc Mező; writer of Paul Street Boys Ferenc Molnár; textile factory owners the Goldberger family; and the family of Manfréd Weiss, owner of the Weiss (later Csepel) Works in Csepel (see p. 286). The 400-capacity synagogue was built in the French Gothic (Neo-Gothic) style.

The symbolism of the number 8

Universally, the number eight symbolises cosmic balance. It is used as a symbol of balance in many esoteric traditions, from Asia to Africa (notably among the Dogons in Mali), and to America (Incas) via Europe. In geometry, the octagon represents the intermediate between the square and the circle. It therefore symbolises mediation between heaven and earth. In mathematics, eight symbolises infinity. In the Jewish tradition, it is on the eighth day that circumcision is practised, which symbolises the capacity of the human being to overcome their limited nature by entering into the Alliance with God. And Hanukkah, an eight-day celebration of infinite light, symbolises the capacity for rebirth and resurrection of the Jewish people on a spiritual level.

THE STATUE
OF PÉTER MANSFELD

*A hidden statue for the youngest victim of the 1956
Revolution*

1023 Budapest, Mansfeld Péter park
Bus: 191 – Mansfeld Péter park / Zivatar utca

A few yards from the tomb of Gül baba, near the corner of Apostol utca and Bolyai utca, in the upper part of Mansfeld Péter park, stands an unusual statue almost completely obscured by four thick square columns. The statue is of Péter Mansfeld (1941–1959), remembered as the youngest victim of the retaliation following the 1956 revolution.

During the revolution, Mansfeld joined the Széna tér group of fighters, transporting food and guns.

Among other things, he broke into the villa of László Piros, former minister of internal affairs, and stole a gun. In February 1958, he and his friends kidnapped a policeman in front of the Austrian embassy and took his weapon before setting him free again. Mansfeld was eventually arrested and sentenced to life in prison.

A council of the Supreme Court later imposed the death sentence. They waited a short while until Mansfeld turned 18, then executed him on 21 March 1959. He was 18 years and 11 days old. Placed here in 2004, the statue is the work of Péter Menasági. The figure of the boy is enclosed by four stone columns, symbolising the state that oppressed and ultimately destroyed Mansfeld.

The park has a good view of the city, especially towards Parliament – a prime spot to watch the fireworks show on 20 August.

Another statue of Péter Mansfeld stands in Szabó Ilonka utca.

THE STAIRCASE
OF 'PISTON HOUSE'

Perhaps the most interesting staircases and lifts in the city

1024 Budapest, 17 Margit körút
Sometimes open during European Heritage Days – otherwise, politely ask an inhabitant for access. Please be discreet as this is private property
Tram: 4, 6 – Margit híd, budai hídfő; Bus: 91, 191, 291 – Margit híd, budai hídfő

During the 1930s it was fashionable to build high-end apartment buildings. Not only did it provide profits for the investor company, it was also a declaration of status. Such a house was built in 1937–38 at 15–17 Margit körút by the pension fund of the Weiss Manfréd Works (see also p. 266): In the core of the building, a stylish combination of staircases and lifts is hidden from the street. This construction by the architects Béla Hofstätter and Ferenc Dománý is certainly worth seeing.

Upon entering the building – either through the main gate on Margit körút or through a smaller entrance from the Margit utca side – a short marble-clad corridor flows into a central elliptical block. Additional doors open onto smaller corridors and the servants' entrances to the kitchens. In addition to the staircase, cylindrical glass lifts were built. These are original and still functioning. The ceiling on the top level incorporates a circular glass panel, allowing natural light into the stairwell.

Further works by the two architects include the Dunapark coffee house near Szent István park and the old Lloyd cinema at the end of Hollán Ernő utca.

Weitere Werke der beiden Architekten sind das Kaffeehaus Dunapark in der Nähe des Szent-István-Parks und das alte Lloyd-Kino am Ende der Hollán Ernő utca.

THE FACES OF
ST FLORIAN CHAPEL

A 1,700-tonne building that was raised 140cm!

1027 Budapest, 88 Fő utca
gorogkatbuda.hu
For events and services see website
Tram: 19, 41 – Bem József tér; Bus: 11, 111 – Horvát utca or 109 – Kacsa utca

Built in 1753, the first chapel on this site was dedicated to St Florian, the patron saint of firefighting. It was extended in 1760 and a new steeple was added to the tower in 1856. After the great flood of 1838 (see p. 106), the municipality decided to elevate the banks of the Danube in this area, too. This meant that the level of the road surface became higher than the entrance and the interior of the church. This, in turn, resulted in a higher groundwater level and increased humidity, which affected the walls inside the chapel. Eventually a decision was made to elevate the whole building.

In 1936–37, using iron beams placed into the walls around the building, the 1,700-tonne building was raised by 15 centimetres a day, adding a new layer of bricks in the gap each time. The chapel was ultimately elevated a total of 140 centimetres, which is why the windows on one side seem particularly high.

Following the elevation, both the interior and exterior of the chapel were renovated. The interior works were supervised by Gyula Wälder (architect of the Madách houses), who added Neo-Baroque stucco to the vaults. New wall paintings were created by Jenő Medveczky in the style of the Roman School.

To watch a 1937 newsreel of the elevation of the building, see: filmhiradokonline.hu/watch.php?id=2203

Modern faces in an old church

Alongside the familiar religious figures in the paintings of Jenő Medveczky, it is also possible to pick out some faces belonging to those who took part in the elevation: town councillor Ákos Farkas and parson Bálint Balogh, as well as the secular head of the congregation, Endre Vaszkó, in one painting and municipality committee member Imre Terbócz and engineer Lajos Fridrich in another.

THE HUNGARIAN 'STOCK IM EISEN'

Memento of a strange old smith's habit from Vienna

1011 Budapest, corner of Iskola utca and Vám utca
Metro: M2 – Batthyány tér

At the corner of Iskola utca and Vám utca is a strange metal structure in a metal cage with an inscription above.

Upon closer inspection, the metallic structure, which looks like a piece of wood with branches, becomes even more peculiar – there seem to be nails hammered into it. Some nailheads are larger, with names or monograms inscribed on them.

The inscription above the structure is a replica of the Buda 'Stock im Eisen', a wooden piece created at the beginning of the 19th century that stood there until the 1960s.

The original piece that inspired this metal replica used to stand here and served as a sign for a bakery.

There used to be one piece in Pest and one in Buda. Both originals can now be seen in Kiscelli Museum (see p. 162). They followed an old tradition: As smiths passed through the city, they were asked to hammer a nail into the tree trunk, until the nailheads finally covered the trunk completely.

The tradition originated from Vienna, where the original 'Stock im Eisen' can still be seen (see *Secret Vienna*, from the same publisher). Originally created in 1533, it has been in Stock-im-Eisen-Platz since 1891.

Locksmiths going to Vienna were supposed to hammer a nail into the tree trunk in memory of a legendary locksmith master. This practice was supposed to prevent or cure certain diseases.

RUBIK'S CUBE SCULPTURE ⑥

One of the many 'mini statues' in Budapest

1011 Budapest, close to Batthyány tér
kolodkoart.com
Tram: 19, 41 – Halász utca (and many others)

By the stairs leading toward the lower wharf of the Danube, close to the end of Vám utca, a small sculpture of a Rubik's Cube often goes unnoticed by passers-by. It is the work of sculptor Mihály (Mihajlo) Kolodko and is part of a greater group of so-called mini sculptures.

Born in Ungvár in 1978, Kolodko moved to Budapest in 2017. In addition to his traditional sculpted works, he began placing mini statues of only a few centimetres around the city. You can find them in various little niches, corners, on fences or integrated into walls. Unfortunately, the statues sometimes go astray, but then a new one will appear, so the list below should not be considered final; it is more a snapshot of the current situation.

The statues are generally welcomed by the people of Budapest. Sometimes a figure is even given a hat or scarf to keep it warm in winter!

Other mini statues have been placed on the promenades of Kőbánya-Újhegy estates (Újhegyi sétány, in the 10th district), but those are by Antal Plank, not Kolodko.

The world-famous Rubik's Cube was invented in 1974 by Ernő Rubik, a Hungarian sculptor and professor of architecture. Close to 500 million have been sold worldwide, with about 200 million between 1980 and 1983, making it the world's bestselling puzzle game.

Other mini statues by Mihály Kolodko in Budapest

– Harry Houdini: The illusionist was born Erik Weisz in Csengery utca but became famous in the US as Houdini. His mini statue, on the first floor of the K11 Art and Cultural Centre (11 Király utca), depicts him in chains.

– Kermit the frog (in the middle of Szabadság tér, next to the entrance of the underground parking lot and coffee house): This is a replica, with the original in Perecseny, in the Subcarpathian region of Ukraine. Eating frogs' legs became a tradition in Perecseny after POWs from Napoleon's army were held there.

– Franz (Ferenc) Liszt: In 2011, on the 200th anniversary of his birth, a statue named after the composer was placed at the Franz Liszt International Airport. He is in the bus stop, sitting on his luggage, as if waiting for a flight. A small airplane was placed in front of the figure, made of music manuscript paper – symbolically combining music and flight in a few centimetres. This is a replica, with the original in Ungvár.

– Dead squirrel: This strange piece can be found by the entrance to the Kieselbach Gallery on the corner of Szent István körút and Falk Miksa utca. The figure refers to 'Bidibidobidiboo', a 1996 installation by Maurizio Cattelan in which a squirrel commits suicide. Perhaps the motive for the fatal act can be uncovered by Lieutenant Columbo, whose statue is just a few metres away.

– Tivadar Herzl: Tivadar Herzl was a Hungarian-Austrian writer, journalist, politician and the father of modern Zionism. He was born in Dohány utca, close to the synagogue, and his mini statue sits on a cable post opposite. Visitors often place a small pebble on the statue in his memory.

– Chequered rabbit (near the upper station of the Sikló – funicular railway): The cartoon episodes begin with the rabbit scanning the view from the top of a building through a telescope – google 'kockásfülű nyúl' to see more.

– Teddy Bear (see p. 97)
– Franz Joseph (see p. 115)
– Winnie the Pooh (see p. 245)
– Noah's Arc (see p. 247)
– Meerkat (see p. 255)
– Skála Kópé (see p. 87)
– Beer delivery horses (see p. 303)
– Worm-in-Chief, Sad tank and Elek Mekk (see following double page)

NEARBY

Worm-in-chief mini statue ⑦

The worm from the popular Hungarian cartoon series *A nagy Ho-Ho-Ho-Horgász* has a mini statue by the Danube, not far from the Rubik's Cube, in Bem rakpart, on a stone balustrade of the path overlooking the river.

Sad tank mini statue ⑧

The military vehicle has its gun barrel bent downwards. It is also on the stone fence in Bem rakpart. Somebody tried to steal it in 2018, but it was repaired and reinstated in early 2019.

Elek Mekk mini statue ⑨

At the bottom of a stairway in Széll Kálmán tér is the figure of Elek Mekk, with a screwdriver in one hand and a piece of wood in the other. The wood is engraved with the former name of the square: Moszkva tér. Elek Mekk is a goat from a Hungarian animation – a jack-of-all-trades who rarely completes a job successfully.

EUROPE GROVE

Trees from 29 cities in one place

1015 Budapest, Európa liget
Bus: 16, 16A, 116 – Bécsi kapu tér or Mátray utca

Just outside Bécsi kapu (Vienna Gate) in the Castle District, there is a small park called Europe Grove. When Budapest celebrated the 100th anniversary of the unification of Pest, Buda, and Óbuda in September 1972, one of the events held was an international conference. It was attended by representatives from 29 European capital cities – each was asked to donate one tree to be planted in this park. Placed among the trees are stones bearing the names of each city.

A statue was erected at the entrance to the grove in 2014. It depicts St Hedvigis (*Jadwiga* in Polish) and Wladislaw II Jagello as ancient Egyptian rulers. Beyond the trees runs a 16th-century segment of castle wall, while within the grove is a charming statue of a bear and a fox – figures from the stories of Zsigmond Sebők.

> Since the original trees were planted, six have been replaced.

THE FLYING NUN SCULPTURE

'It's a street sign. Her skirt flying in the air, decently covering her ankles.'

1014 Budapest, corner of Országház utca / Nándor utca
Bus: 16, 16A, 116 – Kapisztrán tér

In the Castle District, at the corner of Országház utca and Nándor utca, a strange sculpture shows a nun flying in the air. In the 18th century, Clarisse nuns (of the Order of Saint Clare) moved to the building on this corner. After the dissolution of the order in 1782, parliamentary assemblies and extravagant balls were held here – hence the name of the street, *Országház utca* (Parliament Street). The late-Baroque façade and salon were both designed by Franz Anton Hildebrandt.

A memorial plaque to the nuns was to be placed here in 1977, but Hungarian sculptor Miklós Melocco chose a less ordinary solution. It is hard to define his artwork: The figure is depicted in the traditional clothing of the Clarisses, but it is neither relief nor statue. On the belt of the figure, a tiny detail of Latin text can be spotted. Melocco described the artwork as follows: 'It's a street sign. Her skirt flying in the air decently covering her ankles, is on one side of the house, her upper body with a devout face, closed eyes and hands clasped in prayer 'grows' out of the other side of the corner. She flies through the walls. It's jolly, it's good to think of.'*

Tibor Wehner: Melocco Miklós. Helikon Publishing House, Budapest, 2005.

THE HOUSE NUMBER
OF 5 BÉCSI KAPU TÉR

The oldest house number of the Castle District

1014 Budapest, 5 Bécsi kapu tér
Bus: 16, 16A, 116 – Bécsi kapu tér

In the Castle District, 5 Bécsi kapu tér has two house numbers. One is on the right side of the main gate with the number '5', and another is a hand-painted marking above the gate itself: 'N 148'. The official number is n°5, which indeed looks more official, but the N 148 is not there by chance – it is a rare witness of the old numbering system of Budapest, based on a census taken in 1784.

House numbers already existed in the Middle Ages, but they were not organised by street. As in today's Venice, they were organised by district and were called 'numero'.

Every now and then, as new buildings appeared and plots were either combined or split, the numbering had to be revised. Hence, it was more practical to paint the numbers on the houses than carve them into stone.

The decree on the census, issued by emperor Joseph II in 1784, also ordered the renumbering of the houses. Many Hungarian nobles protested against the idea, and Joseph II finally withdrew the decree in 1790.

It was only after another reform in 1874 that the houses were numbered by street, not by district. This allowed for a more stable system, as not all the houses of a district had to be renumbered due to new construction, but only the ones in the given street (if needed).

Other old numbers

The house at 8 Bécsi kapu tér features a number 30 carved into stone above the gate that is not a house number – it is the remaining piece of a larger stone which read '1930', referring to the year of the building's renovation.

The colourful facade of 14 Tárnok utca was renovated from 1950 to 1953 after being damaged in the Second World War. During the restoration, the number 114 was found next to the door on the right. Sometime later, when the facade was renewed again, the number 114 was repainted in a somewhat different style. If the original number was painted on the wall at the same time as the yellow and red of the facade, it is the oldest house number of the city, dated around 1520.

FRESCOES OF
THE NATIONAL ARCHIVES

The history of Hungary painted on walls

1014 Budapest, 2–4 Bécsi kapu tér
+36 1 211 2712
mnl.gov.hu/mnl/ol/epuletseta
leveltarlatogatas@mnl.gov.hu
Guided tours for groups only, reservation needed at least two weeks in advance
See also (in Hungarian): mnl.gov.hu/mnl/ol/epuletlatogatas
Bus: 16, 16A, 116 – Bécsi kapu tér

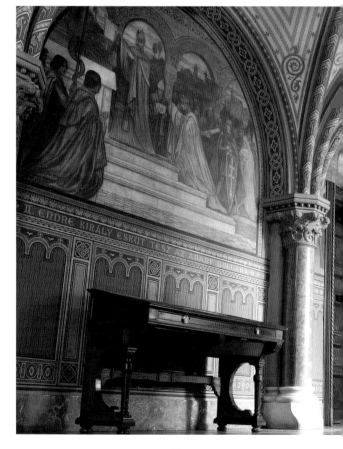

In the Castle District, few people know the spectacular National Archives building can be visited with a booking.

It has beautiful interiors, delicate glazed windows and wall paintings along the corridors, boardroom, research room and staircase.

Among them, the paintings by Andor Dudits depict scenes from Hungarian history. In several cases, figures from the early 1900s can be identified: A knight in armour bears the face of Minister of Culture Kuno Klebelsberg, while two other figures look like Dudits and architect Samu Pecz.

Paintings along the staircase also show historic scenes: the settlement of Hungarians in the Carpathian basin; the foundation of the abbey in Pannonhalma; the acceptance of the Golden Bull; and the inauguration ceremony of the Chain Bridge.

The sequence ends in the 'present' of the 1920s.

Coats of arms of the major towns and cities of old Hungary are pictured in the stained-glass windows by Miksa Róth. During the Second World War, the windows were stored in the cellars to protect them from bomb damage.

In 1723 a law was passed ordering public documents to be stored in a national archive (archivum regni). Yet, the (old) National Archives was not set up until 1756 and moved to Buda between 1784 and 1785. Originally it documented the work of parliament, but its duties gradually became more numerous and the archive became more accessible to

researchers. This led to the creation of a new National Archives and the need for a large building in which to store its documents. The current site was selected in 1911 and, two years later, the old building was demolished. Construction was delayed by the First World War but eventually completed in 1923, based on plans by Pecz.

Frescoes were restored in the 1970s and the roof rebuilt in the 1980s using tiles from the Zsolnay factory.

The original glass roof over the reading room let in more natural light. Unfortunately, it was lost during reconstruction after the Second World War.

The neo-Romanesque building has four levels in a U-shaped configuration. Storage rooms accommodate documents in the two side wings designed with a lower ceiling height for a good reason: The documents are heavy and the structure would not be able to support more. Also, no ladders are needed, enabling faster handling of the documents. Fire safety is improved by dividing up the areas into smaller sections and using steel doors.

The lost tower

The building originally had a tower with a chimney for the heating system and a water reservoir for fire safety. There were already debates about its necessity during the planning phase: Some considered it superfluous, while architect Alajos Hauszmann thought it vital. He reckoned it negated the need for water pumps in the event of a fire, and the water in the reservoir would be kept from freezing by the heat of the smoke. Architect Samu Pecz was also determined to stick to the original plans. The tower was eventually built, but was seriously damaged in 1944–45. After the war, a new debate began. Dr Kálmán Lux, councillor of the National Committee of Protected Buildings, claimed the tower was 'architectural nonsense' and a 75-metre-high structure was not needed. Also, the modernisation of the heating system rendered the chimney redundant. Finally, amid financial restrictions, reconstruction of the building took place and the tower was left out. The remains of the tower were pulled down in the summer of 1945.

A JEWISH HOUSE OF PRAYER (14)

A beautifully restored Jewish corner and two ancient signs

1014 Budapest, 26 Táncsics Mihály utca
info@btm.hu
Tue–Thu 10am–6pm, Fri 10am–5pm, Sun 10am–6pm
Closed during Jewish holidays
Bus: 16, 16A, 116 – Bécsi kapu tér

Among the old houses in the Castle District, close to Bécsi kapu tér, the house at 26 Táncsics Mihály utca has a hidden secret: a small house of prayer for the Jewish community, with centuries-old wall paintings and gravestones, a reminder of a time in the 15th century when Jews lived in the northern half of the Castle District.

Part of the house was used as a community hall, while the synagogue was in another building. During research into the house in 1964, paintings were discovered on its walls. The entrance to the house of prayer is on the ground floor level of the inner yard.

The first exhibit is a collection of old gravestones from the Middle Ages and the period of Turkish occupation: In the 13th century, there was a Jewish cemetery at the bottom of Castle Hill, in the area where the Castle Tunnel now has its west exit. On the left wall, two large signs are painted in red: a Star of David and a blessing from the 4th Book of Moses (Verses 6:24-26 – *The Lord bless you and keep you; the Lord make his face to shine upon you and be gracious to you; the Lord lift up his*

countenance upon you and give you peace.) The painting on the other wall depicts a bow and arrow, with text from the Song of Hannah in the 1st Book of Samuel. (Verse 2:4 – *The bows of the mighty are broken; and those who stumbled, are girded with strength.*)

The Jews in the Castle District

The first Jews (about a dozen families) arrived in the Castle District with the first settlers in the 13th century: The street that today forms a part of Szent György tér used to be called Judengasse (Jewish Street). This small Jewish quarter was closed in 1360 when the king expelled the Jews from Hungary. On their return to Buda, the Jews settled in the area of Táncsics Mihály utca. Their synagogue was built in 1461 in the late Gothic style, but was destroyed during the siege of Buda. On 2 September 1686, the united Christian armies liberated the Castle District from Turkish occupation. They massacred the Jews in the synagogue and burned down the building. The ruins were discovered by archaeologist László Zolnay in the garden of 23 Táncsics Mihály utca in 1964–65, but they were reburied, although there are plans to excavate them again. Some details of this synagogue are exhibited in the back yard of the house of prayer.

In 2005, the ruins of another synagogue were found and reburied under the street by Fehérvári Gate. The houses are long gone, but parts of some cellars and wells survived, including the mikveh, a small ritual bath in a well (see p. 48).

THE CANNONBALL
OF SAINT GEORGE'S HOTEL

A memory of the 1848-1849 Revolution in one of the most pleasant inner yards of Castle District

1014 Budapest, 4 Fortuna utca
Bus: 16, 16A, 116 – Bécsi kapu tér

During the 1848-1849 revolution, Hungarian general Heinrich Hentzi von Arthurm stayed here, provoking a strong reaction from his opponents: They shot cannonballs at the inn, one of which became stuck in the wall. It was left in place as a memento, although it was replaced during a later reconstruction. An old cannon from the era can also be seen in the yard.

Around the old cannon are some grape vines, two of which are several hundred years old. They are specimens in Buda that survived the phylloxera infestation of 1890 and all the wars of the 20th century. The vines are *Bakator* – the name comes from the Italian *bocca d'oro*, meaning 'golden berry' or *aranybogyó* in Hungarian.

The house was built on the remains of three previous houses. From 1784 to 1868, it was occupied by an inn named Fortuna, which gave its name to the street. The Fortuna Inn had 12 suites, a restaurant, a cafe and billiard room, and stables for 50 horses. In later years, the building was used for private dwellings, an art school and a printing house. Damages from the Second World War were left unrepaired for decades. Then from 1966 to 2004 the Hungarian Museum of Trade and Tourism was located here. Following the museum's move to Óbuda, the building was fully renovated and opened as a hotel and restaurant.

The restaurant area is well worth a look: Its walls and ceilings are richly painted with Baroque floral patterns and birds-of-paradise.

THE HISTORIC REMAINS WITHIN THE HILTON HOTEL

Historic remains hidden behind a 1970s façade

1014 Budapest, 1–3 Hess András tér
Bus: 16, 16A, 116 – Szentháromság tér

From the outside, it's hard to imagine what lies behind the walls of the Hilton Hotel: the spectacular remains of a medieval Dominican abbey, harmoniously integrated into the hotel's recent construction. Built in the 13th century, the abbey belonged to the Dominican Order and stood until the Turkish occupation. The walls of its nave, three windows and the

foundations of its sanctuary are what remained of the original stones. It can be accessed from the area in front of the Fishermen's Bastion, and can be seen through the glass walls of the Lobby Café & Bar.

The 13th-century Saint Nicholas (Szt. Miklós) tower, once an addition to the Dominican church, can also be seen from the outside. In the Middle Ages, the upper section had an octagonal layout, which is reflected in the modern reconstruction. In 1976 a water tank and several antennae were built into the upper section, dictating its ultimate height. A replica of king Matthias' memorial stone in Bautzen was placed on the wall of the tower in 1930.

Parts of the northern wing of the hotel retain stylised versions of the abbey ruins, and the cloister was also rebuilt. Displayed along the cloister are Roman relics and pieces of gravestones from the 14th and 15th centuries. An eight metre-deep well in the middle bears the coats of arms of King Matthias and János Szapolyai. Where original material was missing, it has been substituted with modern materials, such as copper sheets and glass blocks embedded in concrete.

The southern wing features the original façade of a Jesuit college, built between 1688 and 1702 and expanded with an additional storey in 1785. Following the Second World War, only the walls of the main facade remained standing and were incorporated into the hotel building. In order to match the hotel rooms to the old façade, the levels of the rooms were staggered.

Before the Hilton hotel was built in the 1970s, the site was already subject to archaeological research: Historians and archaeologists even took part in the design of the complex.

DE LA MOTTE-BEER PALACE AND ITS ATTIC

A glimpse into the world of 18th-century pharmacy

1014 Budapest, 15 Dísz tér
Guided tours only, see budaivarsetak.hu
Bus 16, 16A, 116, 216 – Dísz tér

The richly decorated walls, the *enfilade* (suite of rooms), kitchen and attic of the small De La Motte-Beer palace at 15 Dísz tér in the Castle District are definitely worth a look: They provide a beautiful glimpse into the world of 18th-century pharmacy. Though the furniture in the rooms is not authentic, the wall decoration is quite something. It's a miracle that the original art could be restored from underneath more than a dozen layers of subsequent paint. Forming the main part of the historical attraction are the winter dining room, the living room (with wall art depicting the Passion of the Christ), a bedroom, a study, and the splendid salon. The paintings in the study refer to the life of János Beer, the son who became a doctor.

Other rooms are just as interesting. The kitchen, much simpler in design, boasts a barrel vault ceiling. Once characteristic of the whole building, it survived later reconstructions only in this room. A few steps further on, a steep staircase leads up to the attic, where dried herbs hint at the old use of this space. As a pharmacist, Beer used the herbs to create his medicines, lotions and deodorants. Most of the beams in the roof structure are more than 200 years old.

In the Middle Ages, three houses stood here, but all were destroyed during the siege of Buda in 1686. The remaining foundations were used in the Baroque era to build two new houses. The De La Motte family moved briefly into one of these in 1760. De la Motte was a lieutenant colonel in the army. The house was sold in 1773 to the royal and military chemist József Beer, and it was he who endowed it with wall paintings along the *enfilade* – the suite of interconnected rooms on the upper level that can be visited today, while the ground floor is mostly occupied by a post office.

THE *MIKVEH*
OF SZENT GYÖRGY TÉR

A hidden mikveh *in the Castle District*

1014 Budapest, Szent György tér
budaivarsetak.hu
Guided group tours only
Bus: 16, 16A, 116 – Dísz tér

Accessible on guided tours (see opposite), deep under the street level, the mikveh of Szent György tér is a long-abandoned well that was once the ritual bath of the local Jewish community.

Once a month, as a purification act, Jewish women were indeed obliged to immerse themselves fully in the water (many were using it on a more irregular basis).

The *mikveh* was always one of the first things to be built in a new Jewish settlement, taking priority even over the synagogue. A walled-up section hides a basin that once held more water. Originally, a wooden staircase led down to the *mikveh*, with a wooden ladder leading into the basin.

Today's Szent György tér was the area where the first Jewish families built their houses, close to Fehérvári Gate, following the fortification of the country after the Mongol invasion of Hungary in 1241–1242. There are no original houses left in the area, but you can visit the cellars and the cave system that has remained partly intact through the

centuries. The cellars were once put to several uses, including food and wine storage, and for hiding from enemies. The wells also provided fresh water for each individual house. One of them is even from King Matthias' time in the 15th century.

The only functioning *mikveh* in modern Budapest is in Kazinczy utca, available only to members of the Jewish community.

For more information on the history of Jews in Budapest, see p. 259.

Geologically, the lowest level is dolomite, covered by a layer of Buda marl – a porous rock containing clay. Above this, there is a layer of sedimentary rock, then a layer of limestone, varying in thickness. Ancient hot water springs created cavities in the upper layers, and these were carved into cellars and wells by the first settlers. Hence the porous, sponge-like structure of the Castle District – which is also why only lightweight public transport buses are allowed there.

THE MARKINGS OF CHAIN BRIDGE

How to measure the water level of the Danube

Buda side of the Chain Bridge
Bus: 16, 16B, 105 – Clark Ádám tér; Tram: 19, 41 – Clark Ádám tér

On the Buda side stone pillar of the Chain Bridge, if you look closely enough, you will notice roman numbers carved into the stone: XI, X, IX etc. On their right, different lines are carved as well and, on their right, another set of roman numbers can also be seen.

Those two systems were designed in the 19th century to measure the level of the water of the Danube.

The first, using Viennese feet (*bécsi láb*, equalling 0.31608 metres), was carved in 1850. Shortly after, other figures were carved beside it, using the metric system.

Both were supposed to have the same '0' point, but the metric marking is actually 8.4 millimetres higher, and since 1850, the gradual sinking of the pillars into the Danube (78 millimetres in a hundred years) made the measurements inexact.

A new meter was created in 1817 under the Vigadó tér boat station. After an upgrade in 1988, this meter was declared the official provider of water level data.

NEARBY
The floodometer
1011 Budapest, 2 Bem rakpart

Just north of Chain Bridge, an ornate grey cabinet stands between the tram tracks and the pavement. The old-looking structure encases a modern display where anyone can check the current water level of the Danube.

Made from cast iron from the foundry of Antal Oetl (the old factory building is now home to the Foundry Museum), the cabinet was installed around 1913-1915. Originally its four sides were equipped with a floodometer, a thermometer, a barometer and a clock. Unfortunately, over the years, the equipment broke down or was damaged. It was last renovated in 2017, when a digital display was installed in the grey cabinet, replacing the former mechanic displays.

The plaque of the very first floodometer

The very first instrument to measure the water level of the Danube in Budapest was installed in the area where the Castle Garden Bazaar now stands. Completely renewed in 1817, it was connected to the wooden pipes that carried water to Castle Hill. It was used in October 1863 for the last time, when it defined the '0' point of the meter carved on Chain Bridge, and was deconstructed in 1877, together with the water works. Its only visible memory is a plaque on a wall of the Castle Bazaar (Várbazár or Várkertbazár in Hungarian).

JÓZSEF GRUBER
WATER RESERVOIR

A piano full of fresh water

Gellért Hill, 1016 Budapest, Víztározó köz
vizmuvek.hu
Visits are possible only on special occasions such as World Water Day in March,
organised by Budapest Waterworks
Bus: 8E, 108E, 110, 112, 178 – Sánc utca

Although the green side of Gellért Hill offers a beautiful panorama over the city, few inhabitants know that there is a huge reservoir of fresh water under their feet. Accessible on special occasions, it offers a very spectacular interior which rewards visitors for their efforts.

Outside, the buttresses of the reservoir were formed to look like rocks, in order to blend in with its natural environment within the park. Invis-

ible from both the Pest side and the Castle District, the hidden entrance gate gives way to a small exhibition that details the history and the present water supply network in Budapest, from the earliest wells to the current system of automatised water reservoirs. Right next to the exhibition hall, a narrow corridor with glass windows allows for a glimpse of one of the reservoirs and the series of supporting columns.

The water comes from the Danube through wells and flows into the reservoirs, the largest of which was built inside this hill between 1974 and 1980. There are two basins with a storage capacity of 2 x 40,000 cubic metres of water held within reinforced concrete walls (35 cm thick). Designing this facility presented a particular problem: how to achieve a continuous flow of water and prevent stagnation. The issue was overcome by using a special basin shaped like a grand piano, a method first tested on a smaller scale when building the reservoir in Rákosszentmihály. Research work was led by József Gruber, after whom the Gellért Hill facility was named.

The lower part of the columns inside the basins were cast together with the foundations. The concrete was poured continuously to ensure the whole foundation remained a single structure, minimising the possibility of leaks. A total of 25 mixers transported raw concrete to the site for 41 consecutive days and nights, while more than 200 workers built 50 cubic metres of concrete into the structure daily. Walls and columns followed and a concrete ceiling was added. A steel layer protects the top of the structure from the roots of the plants above.

GARDEN OF PHILOSOPHY ON GELLÉRT HILL

Statues embracing major religions

On Gellért Hill, near Hegyalja út, Sánc utca and Orom utca
Open all year round
Bus: 8E, 110, 112 – Sánc utca

Erected on Gellért Hill in 2001 by the sculptor Nándor Wagner (1922–1997), the Garden of Philosophy is an unusual group of statues that was gifted to the city of Budapest in 1997.

Born in Hungary, Wagner lived in Sweden from 1956 and in Japan from 1967. Intrigued by different cultures, throughout his life he looked for commonalities in religions and philosophies – universal messages rather than differences. His search led to the creation of this artwork.

A sphere, the symbol of 'allness' (whether God, Allah, or Kamisama), sits within a circle. Five figures look in towards the centre of the circle: Abraham, Akhenaten (Amenhotep IV), Jesus, Buddha and Laozi, representing five of the world's major religions. Three more figures stand

in a row outside the circle: Saint Francis of Assisi, Daruma (Boddhi Dharma) and Mahatma Gandhi, who amended the teachings of the world religions. Together with the central sphere, they form a triangle.

In 2007, the three outer figures were stolen, so Wagner's widow, Aki-yama Chiyo, made the casting moulds available and the statues were cast again. Since 2009 the composition has been complete again, making it a perfect place to pause and reflect – above the city and under the sky.

There is another Wagner statue just outside Bécsi kapu in the Castle District. The circular sculpture is titled 'Mother Earth' and lies in the grass on the corner of Ostrom utca and Lovas út.

Nándor Wagner created another similar group of statues in the Garden of Philosophy in the Nakano district of Tokyo (see also *Secret Tokyo* from the same publisher). This Japanese version was inaugurated on 4 December 2009, the 140th anniversary of dip-lomatic relations being established between Hungary and Japan.

FAMINE ROCK

A natural signal of climate change

North of Szabadság bridge on the Buda side
Metro: M4 – Szent Gellért tér

Looking north from the Buda end of Szabadság bridge, the Danube rarely presents anything out of the ordinary. However, if the water level drops particularly low, a rock formation will surface. Named Ínség-szikla (Famine Rock or Hunger Rock), it appears only when the level reaches 90 100 centimetres, something that has recently happened several times: in 2011, 2015, 2016, 2018 and 2022.

Historically, when the water was this low, fishing was practically impossible, transportation was severely restricted and drought conditions affected agriculture, causing multiple economic problems, hence the name of the rock.

In terms of geology, the rock is part of Gellért Hill, which is itself part of a larger formation of 220-million-year-old dolomite that rose between 34 and 59 million years ago. Further sedimentation and geological activity resulted in several layers of rock: The Famine Rock is silicified Eocene sandstone, but clay layers can also be found in the area.

Centuries ago, before the road was built between the hill and the river, large rocks would fall from the cliff into the Danube. Along the Buda side of the Danube, evidence of the formation can still be witnessed: South of the bridge, swirling water is created by the presence of the rocks.

The Buda pillar was built partly on the formation, and in 2009 it was partially drilled to allow the M4 metro line to pass under the Danube.

THE PLAQUE OF THE FORMER HYDROPLANE STATION

Commemorating a hydroplane station

1118 Budapest, Szent Gellért tér
Metro - M4 - Szent Gellért tér, Tram 47, 49 - Szent Gellért tér, bus 7, 133E -
Szent Gellért tér

On the Buda side of Szabadság Bridge, a discreet stone plaque commemorates the hydroplane station that operated from 1923 to
1926 at Gellért tér, in the heart of the city, right by the bridge's Buda

side. Tickets were sold at the reception desk of Hotel Gellért – one of the largest hotels in Budapest at that time, attracting a lot of famous and rich visitors. The fleet consisted of Junkers F13 planes, the world's first all-metal transport aircraft, that landed and took off from the Danube itself.

In 1922, after the ban on all flights in Hungary (following the Treaty of Trianon peace agreement in 1920) was eased, civil aircraft could fly again. The Hungarian count Endre Jankovich-Bésán teamed up with the German Junkers company to set up a joint venture in 1923: Aeroexpress was born with flights to lake Balaton and Vienna.

Mainly due to the political circumstances, the company ceased operating just three years later: Despite the granting of initial licences, in the end they could only set up international flights to Germany and Austria, which proved to be not enough to make the business viable.

The fastest pilot to cross the Atlantic: 13h50min in 1931

The company's most famous pilot was György Endresz who served in the First World War before joining Aeroexpress and the German Junkers Aircraft Works. His most famous flight was in 1931, with navigator Sándor Magyar: They took off from Newfoundland and reached the coast of Ireland in less than 14 hours, despite heavy fog and issues with their compass. They had planned to land their Lockheed Sirius (named 'Justice for Hungary') at Mátyásföld airport in Budapest, but due to severe weather and the consequent changes in route, they were forced to land near Felcsút instead. They flew 5770 kilometres in only 25 hours and 20 minutes, breaking three world records on the way: They were the fastest to cross the Atlantic, reaching Ireland in 13 hours and 50 minutes; they reached the highest average speed (230km/h) on a long distance flight; and they flew deeper into the European continent than any previous flight. Endresz and Magyar were only the 15th in the world to fly over the Atlantic Ocean.

UNDER GELLÉRT BATH TOUR

The origin of the hot water of the Gellert Bath

1118 Budapest, 4 Kelenhegyi út
imagine.hu
Guided tours only, see website
Metro: M4 – Szent Gellért tér

Although the Gellért Bath is world famous, not only do few visitors know, but few Budapest inhabitants know that it is possible, on a guided tour, to access the spaces below the bath, occupied by machinery, equipment and a long corridor that connects to a small cave. The visit also provides access to the source of the thermal waters that come from an old well, 15 metres below Gellért Square.

The benefits of the local thermal water were enjoyed by people as early as the 15th century. The local medicinal mud was already famous in the Middle Ages, hence the old name Sáros-fürdő (Mud Bath). Due to the increasing number of travellers in the 19th century, the bath's popularity increased significantly, leading to the construction of a first building which was demolished when Szabadság Bridge was constructed in 1894, together with the extension of the quay.

The current building incorporating Gellért Bath and Hotel Gellért was opened in 1918. However, Gellért Square was also built up during the same period, pushing the spring underground. Unfortunately, the water of the spring combined with the water from the Danube, removing the qualities of the water, which meant that a new thermal spring had to be found for the bath.

Inside Gellért Hill, a tunnel roughly a kilometre long was therefore built between Gellért Bath, Rudas Bath and Rácz Bath in the 1960s to channel other thermal springs into Gellért Bath. The tunnel even had a narrow gauge railway line and included pipes for the district heating network (piped hot water), providing heating from Kelenföld Power Station (see p. 200) to the Castle District. It was also intended to be a bomb shelter during the Cold War era, although it was never actually used. During construction of the tunnel, a smaller cave was discovered under the cave church, called Aragonit Cave or Cauliflower Cave.

THE LIBRARY OF
THE TECHNICAL UNIVERSITY

A must-see hidden treasure

1111 Budapest, 4-6 Budafoki út
omikk.bme.hu
Mon–Fri 9am–8pm with an annual ticket
Open days in November; Guided tours during European Heritage Days in
September
Metro: M4 – Szent Gellért tér; Tram: 17, 19, 41, 47, 47B, 48, 49, 56, 56A –
Gárdonyi tér

With its Neo-Gothic arches, large windows and classical furniture, the library of the Technical University looks as if it had just arrived from a Harry Potter film. The historic university campus is a must-see hidden treasure of the city, and its gem is clearly the library reading room.

Despite being the architect of the Market Hall on Fővám tér and the National Archives in Castle District, Samu Pecz is not particularly well known. He first drafted plans for the main reading library of the Technical University (located behind the central 'K' building) in 1905, and construction was completed by 1909.

The roof is furnished with tiles from the Zsolnay factory, while the original glass works were supplied by Miksa Róth. A closed corridor known as Sóhajok hídja (Bridge of Sighs) connects the main building to the T-shaped library, within which there are three distinct areas, each with a specific function: a reading room, areas for processing, and storage – the rack system was produced by the Schlick Iron Foundry and Machine Factory Co. It is well worth the short walk from Gellért tér.

Inside the library, an immense granite staircase connects the lower levels with the upper corridor of the bridge. The reading room is about 400 square metres and can accommodate 200 readers. The arches of its 11-metre-high ceiling are supported by a dozen marble columns. In 1913 a secco was painted above the main entrance. Measuring 12 by 8 metres, it depicted the evolution of mankind through more than 80 portraits. Sadly, this is no longer visible.

When Emperor Franz Joseph visited the university in 1910, a six-metre-tall Carrara marble statue of the Emperor and Empress Elisabeth was gifted by the prime minister of Hungary to the university. The plinth was designed by Imre Steindl, architect of the Parliament building. Additional supporting pillars were needed in the basement to support the weight of the statue, which was placed in the centre of the library. After the Second World War, the statue of Elisabeth was taken to Epreskert (see p. 70).

THE CHURCH
OF HUNGARIAN SAINTS

A church that was the Vatican pavilion of a World Expo which never happened

1117 Budapest, 1 Magyar Tudósok körútja
magyarszentektemploma.hu (check for services)
Tram: 4, 6 – Petőfi híd, budai hídfő; Bus 153, 212 – Petőfi híd, budai hídfő

In the early 1990s, the World Exposition Expo '95 was to be held in Budapest. Later changed to Expo '96, to be held in Budapest and Vienna, the project was eventually cancelled due to economic difficulties in the country, although some of the necessary construction had already got underway. Following the cancellation, the Catholics decided to build the Vatican pavilion anyway – from the start it was intended to function as a church after the Expo, in order to serve the area and the youth at the nearby universities. Designed by architects Mihály Balázs and Ferenc Török, the church opened in August 1996. The pavilion is made up of two sections connected by a wooden gate: a central, domed hall, and the elongated parish building (including assembly halls and offices). Between the dome and the gate, a tower-like wall incorporates three bells.

On the cross, the figure of Jesus was carved from a 70-year-old pear tree that died in the same year the church was consecrated. A plaque beneath the organ commemorates Pope John Paul II, who blessed the foundation stone.

The road network of the Infopark, the Rákóczi Bridge and the Tüskecsarnok sports hall are further memories of the Expo that never happened: The C-shaped road would have been the main road of the area. Rákóczi Bridge was opened in 1995, but the Tüskecsarnok sports hall was only opened in 2014.

Central Pest

SCHIFFER VILLA

A splendid little gem in the city

Hungarian Museum of Customs and Taxation History
1063 Budapest, 19/B Munkácsy utca
+36 (1) 472 6342
muzeum@nav.gov.hu
Mon–Thu 8am–3:30pm, Fri 8am–1:30pm
Guided tours available, call or email for bookings
Metro: M1 – Bajza utca; Trolley Bus: 72 – Rippl-Rónai utca or Munkácsy
Mihály utca

Concealed among the smaller streets of the 6th district, unknown even to most locals, the beautiful Schiffer villa is a splendid little gem in the city. Not only is the beauty of the villa to be admired (the original stained glass windows, wooden interiors and staircase), but you can also discover a museum presenting the Hungarian history of customs and taxation.

Built in 1910–12, the villa was based on designs by architect József Vágó, who was also responsible for the Gutenberg House, Gresham Palace and the Árkád Bazár building (see p. 108). It was built for Miksa Schiffer, a wealthy entrepreneur and railway engineer. The recurring theme of the decoration is the rebirth of the arts, creating a new harmony between people and nature. Most of the interiors were designed by Vágó, including furniture, majolica, textiles, and lighting. Zsolnay ceramics depict flora and fauna, while geometric patterns reflect the influence of the Wiener Werkstätte art school. Many items also feature a small SM monogram: the initials of Miksa Schiffer (in Hungary, the family name is written first).

The ground floor was the public area, including the hall, dining room, salons and a study, while the upper level was reserved for the family. In the cellar were the housekeeper's quarters, along with a kitchen, a boiler room and a billiard room. The hall remains the most authentic room: Its large Károly Kernstock stained glass window depicting the lost 'ideal world' was restored in the 1980s. On the wall, Kernstock's painting has Schiffer at its centre. A Carrara marble pool of flowers (by Vilmos Fémes Beck) and a white marble seated male nude (by sculptor Miklós Ligeti) can also be seen in the hall.

After the Second World War, a new wing was added to the villa in the rear yard and the upper rooms were divided up. The Hungarofruct company had its headquarters here for decades. In 1994 the building was given to the Customs and Excise Authority and restoration work began. A year later, the Museum of Hungarian Customs and Taxation History was opened. Especially interesting are the artefacts related to the customs in the harbour of Fiume (today Rijeka): These include uniforms of excise officers, typewriters, coats of arms and old photographs.

EPRESKERT ART COLONY

A haven for art

1062 Budapest, 41 Bajza utca
mke.hu
Open during events only (see website)
Metro: M1 – Bajza utca; Trolley Bus: 72 – Bajza utca

Bordered by Bajza utca, Szondi utca, Munkácsy Mihály utca and Kmety György utca, Epreskert ('Mulberry Garden' in Hungarian) was an artists' colony in Budapest at the end of the 19th and beginning of the 20th centuries. Mulberry trees were grown here until the 1870s. More plots were created as the city expanded, and the first artist to move to this area was the sculptor Adolf Huszár, who built his Neo-Renaissance atelier on a plot donated by the municipal council.

In 1883 the Hungarian Academy of Fine Arts (now the Hungarian University of Fine Arts) occupied the north section. Over the following decades, artists moved into new ateliers: The sculptor of the Millenium Monument on Heroes' Square, György Zala, and the painter of the enormous cyclorama 'Arrival of the Hungarians' (exhibited in Ópusztaszer), Árpád Feszty, were among the residents. After the First World War many ateliers were dismantled or replaced. During the Second World War, the site was bombed and part of it was later seized by the neighbouring Soviet embassy.

What remains today are the gardens, the centre of which is occupied by the calvary that used to stand on Kálvária tér – the sculptor Alajos Stróbl saved it from demolition in 1893 and reconstructed it here piece by piece. The gardens have become a haven for art: Stone works from Matthias Church in the Castle District were brought here by Stróbl when the church was rebuilt; there is a statue of the Hungarian painter Bertalan Székely by György Oszvald (1930) and a replica of King Matthias' bust, commissioned by Stróbl. Stróbl's own atelier is guarded by a gypsum study of a horse for the statue of St Stephen in front of the Fishermen's Bastion.

As Epreskert belongs to the university, there is no public access, but there are many events during which the gardens and some of the ateliers can be visited.

THE MASONIC SYMBOLS
OF 45 PODMANICZKY UTCA

The former headquarters of the Symbolic Grand Lodge of Hungary

Mystery hotel
1064 Budapest, 45 Podmaniczky utca
mysteryhotelbudapest.com
Trolley Bus: 73 – Ferdinánd híd (Izabella utca)

Now a luxurious hotel, the building at 45 Podmaniczky utca hides many discreet symbols on its façade that reflect its former use as the headquarters of the Symbolic Grand Lodge of Hungary. The keystones of the ground floor window arches feature Egyptian-style female Hermes figures, while a sphinx figure highlights the avant-corps of the main façade. (Ancient Egypt has always inspired Freemasonry, following the belief that it was one of the major places of wisdom and knowledge). A large globe supported by four owls (symbols of wisdom and sometimes of the gift of clairvoyance) dominates the corner of the roof. Signs of the zodiac also run around its circumference and the Eye of Providence (symbolising the fact that everything a human being does in life is observed by the Great Architect of the Universe, and will have direct consequences) looks down from the top. Other masonic symbols can be seen on the building, including the well-known square and compass appearing on stone vases (see p. 75).

The building also boasts many symbols in the large halls inside, and these can now be seen by the public, which was not the case in the past. The former great hall, now serving as a restaurant, is found on the fourth floor. The black and white chequered floor (which reminds us that all our daily actions are a mix of good and bad), the ceiling decorated with stars (upward aspiration) are, for instance, important features in the decoration.

Freemasons in Hungary

The first Hungarian Masonic lodge was established in 1774 in Bratislava, with Ferenc Kazinczy and Ignác Martinovics among its members. Banned in 1795, Freemasons began to flourish again after the Austro-Hungarian Compromise of 1867.

The Symbolic Grand Lodge of Hungary was formed in 1886 from the merger of two organisations: the Blue Lodge and the Scottish Ritual Grand Orients.

From that time until 1919, Hungarian Freemasonry flourished: Almost 11,000 Freemasons worked in almost a hundred lodges, including figures such as Endre Ady, József Balassa, György Bölöni, Ignotus, Károly Kernstok, András Mechwart, Sándor Wekerle, Dezső Kosztolányi, István Ferenc Pulszky, Elek Benedek, Géza Kresz, Jenő Heltai, Ottó Bláthy Titusz and many others.

The Symbolic Grand Lodge of Hungarian Freemasons proposed the construction of a lodge house in 1890. They received 12 different entries from which that of Vilmos Ruppert was accepted. Ruppert was himself a Freemason, as he was a member of the Old Calls Lodge. The building was finally handed over solemnly in 1896. The most important venue was the great sanctuary on the fourth floor (also called Temple or Atelier by various lodges) as it was one of the most important halls of the building (stained glass windows by Miksa Róth and portraits in the Grand Master's office by Mór Than). Today it houses the hotel restaurant. During the First World War, the building served as a field hospital and was operated by the Grand Lodge. Nationalised in 1919, after the former Republic of Councils in Hungary and later the Interior Minister of Hungary, Mihály Dömötör, had formally banned the activities of the Freemasons, the house was then occupied in May 1920 by the Hungarian Association of National Defence. After the Second World War, Freemasons once again used the building for a short time until 1947, when the Interior Ministry occupied it until the regime change in 1989. It then stood empty for decades until 2018, when the building was transformed into a hotel.

The Masonic symbolism of the square and compass

The square, which is used to check angles in construction, also teaches 'to act with rectitude, in accordance with the Masonic rule and to harmonise one's conduct with the principles of morality and virtue'. Symbolising the Freemason who works on himself going from rough stone to cut stone, the square is often equated with matter and indicates 'rectitude in action'.

The compass, with its variable spacing, symbolises the mind and denotes 'measure in research'.

A careful observer will notice that, although they are often represented together, they are not always positioned in the same way.

The position of the square on the compass refers to the first grade, that of Apprentice: At this stage, matter (square) still takes precedence over mind (compass).

The square and compass, when crossed, refer to the second degree of Freemasonry: The Companion grade, a degree of evolution where matter and spirit are balanced, a necessary condition for attaining spiritual enlightenment.

When the compass is placed on the square, it indicates that the spirit (spirituality) has overcome matter (profane), an initiatory progression represented in the Masonic hierarchy by the third grade of Master Mason.

THE ROYAL WAITING ROOM
OF NYUGATI STATION

④

From where the Habsburgs once travelled to the Palace of Gödöllő

1065 Budapest, Nyugati tér
mavrailtours.hu
Check website for events organised by MÁV Rail Tours, also European Heritage Days in September or the Night of Museums in June
Metro: M3 – Nyugati pályaudvar

Built in 1877, Nyugati railway station replaced an earlier building from 1846, and was a gem in the Austro-Hungarian crown. Trains left from here to the Royal Palace of Gödöllő, and to Vienna, so a truly royal waiting room was built for the exclusive use of the royal family. It had a separate entrance on the arrival side of the main hall, and from within a large gate allowed quick access to the royal train. The two salons are in need of renovation, but are magnificent nevertheless and can be visited during special events.

The small wall lamps on either side of the main gate were topped by crowns, indicating the function of the halls beyond. Above the gate, a Latin inscription reads *VIRIBUS UNITIS* – the slogan of emperor Franz Joseph, meaning 'with united forces'. It was also the name of a battleship, an award, and was also inscribed on the edge of coins during the monarchy's reign. Originally, the royal waiting area consisted of a great salon, a smaller salon for Empress Elisabeth (Sisi), a meeting room for Franz Joseph, two changing rooms, and rooms for a guard and a servant. On the wall of the great salon, the coats of arms of the counties of Arad, Máramaros, Heves, Bihar, Fehér, Pozsony, and Trencsén are displayed, indicating the destinations of trains departing from this station in 1877. The statues of Franz Joseph and Sisi were later replaced with those of István Széchenyi and Gábor Baross. In Sisi's room there are large mirrors on the walls, visually enlarging the space. It was connected to a small garden with a fountain in its centre: The garden still exists but without its fountain.

Famous visitors in the past have included Prince Charles, Khrushchev, Tito and Richard Nixon.

PINBALL EXHIBITION

Play unlimited pinball!

1137 Budapest, 18 Radnóti Miklós utca
flippermuzeum.hu/en
Wed–Fri 4pm–12 midnight, Sat 2pm–12 midnight, Sun 10am–10pm
Metro: M3 – Nyugati pályaudvar or Lehel tér

Secluded in a basement at 18 Radnóti Miklós utca since it opened in 2014, the Pinball Exhibition, also known as the Flipper Museum, has become relatively popular with foreign visitors although it is fairly unknown among locals. In addition to the collection of pinballs, the main attraction is that for the price of the entrance fee to the museum, you can play for an unlimited time.

Long before the internet and online gaming took over, pinball was widespread. The machines inevitably vanished and are rarely seen today, but in this basement there are over a hundred of them. The machines were collected by Balázs Pálfi, whose passion for pinball began in the 1980s, which was pinball's golden era. Pálfi acquired his collection from across the globe: The largest, called Hercules, came from the United States in 2015 and features balls the size of those on a billiard table. It can only be played during the Arcadia exhibition (see arcadiafest.hu). During this time, visitors are taken back to the 1980s, when pubs and bars were full of pinball games. It is organised once a year in larger locations than the Radnóti utca basement, allowing for a much wider range of games to be tried, and enabling participation in retro computer game tournaments, too.

The origin of the name pinball

Older machines from the 1930s include actual pins instead of rubber bumpers, hence the English name for these games. The oldest example is a bagatelle from 1871.

As well as pinball, classic arcade games like Space Invaders and Mortal Kombat can also be enjoyed.

SECCO OF 'THE WORKERS' STATE' ⑥

A large-scale communist painting discreetly criticising the regime …

1055 Budapest, 19 Széchenyi rakpart
The secco can be seen from the security desk
Tram: 2, 4, 6 – Jászai Mari tér

On the Danube side, the office building of the Hungarian Parliament features not only a modern facade, but also a rather brave, under-the-radar artwork: a large painting that criticised Kádár's socialist system.

Created between 1968 and 1972 by Aurél Bernáth, the 96-square-metre painting was inaugurated on the 60th birthday of János Kádár. At first glance, it appears to depict 'The Workers' State' and the proletariat. However, on closer inspection, strange details can be spotted.

Contrary to the title, not a single figure is actually working: Some are listening to a speech, some are chatting with each other, one figure is smoking a cigarette, and so on – doing anything but working.

Many of the faces are quite blurred, but a few are rather detailed. A scene shows two people playing chess – one of them resembles János Kádár, the communist leader of Hungary for several decades. Another figure, standing above him, looks like György Aczél (as the cultural leader of the country, he ordered the painting from Aurél Bernáth).

Nearby, a propagandist is delivering a speech to seated workers, but the figure is depicted without a mouth, as if the propaganda speech was meaningless. One of the listeners also appears to be Imre Nagy, the leader of the country during the 1956 revolution, who was executed after the fall of the revolution. It meant that János Kádár – who became the next leader of the country after the execution of Imre Nagy, with support from Moscow – had to see his predecessor's face whenever he went to work …

Also among the audience is the writer Tibor Déry, who was blacklisted in Hungary in the 70s for his antisocialist position.

The artist himself also appears among the figures, as well as several churches in the background, highlighting another forbidden topic of communist propaganda. Not a single red star can be spotted on the entire artwork.

The (re)construction of the building, also known as the 'White House', began in 1947. Its first occupant was the infamous ÁVH, the secret police of the Stalinist regime. Following the abolition of the ÁVH, the building was handed over to the Communist Party in 1961. János Kádár had his offices on the first floor. The building once held more than a million files on the citizens of Hungary.

THE PARLIAMENT LIBRARY

A beautiful reading room rarely visited

1055 Budapest, 1-3 Kossuth Lajos tér
parlament.hu/en/web/orszaggyulesi-konyvtar
Mon–Fri 9am–8pm, Sat 10am–6pm – booking required (see website)
Booking for group visits: latogatas@ogyk.hu
Metro: M2 – Kossuth tér

Founded in 1868 and located here since 1902, the library of the Hungarian Parliament boasts a beautiful reading room that is surprisingly rarely visited by Budapesters or by tourists. To visit the library, you can register for a membership card or arrange a group visit in advance – see the website for details.

The impressive Main Reading Room is 30 metres long and two storeys high. Other than the pine shelves, the interiors are fashioned from Slavonian oak, with wrought iron railings by Sándor Árkay (also responsible for the gates of the New York Palace and the Nyugati Railway Station). Most of the woodwork was produced by Alajos Michl's studio. Leaf-shaped decorations can be found not only in the library, but also throughout the building. Beyond the main entrance (gate XXV on the Danube side), painted wood panels also adorn the ceiling above the information desk. Despite being reupholstered several times, the armchairs are part of the original furnishings of the building and are now over 110 years old.

Designed by architect Imre Steindl to house an increasingly large collection of works, it became a public library in 1952. The decorative main reading room on the Danube side is supplemented by five smaller ones overlooking the square. Two additional reading rooms originally served the upper and lower houses. (Today, the Hungarian Parliament has only one house – however, members of the parliament still often visit the library.) Books and journals kept here span the themes of law, politics and history in Hungary and the rest of the world.

As of 2014, the library had 700,000 volumes, increasing by around 5,000 every year. The oldest book is Werbőczy's Tripartitum, dated 1514. Rarities include the fabulas of Terentius (1550), a Luther Bible from 1569 and the beautifully illustrated Icones Plantarium, published in 14 volumes between 1800 and 1822. Included in the Rare Books and Manuscripts Collection are about 8,000 volumes dated earlier than 1851.

BARBER MUSEUM

*A unique collection of barbers' tools and a great
place to have your hair cut*

1054 Budapest, 64 Bajcsy-Zsilinszky út
borbelymuzeum.hu
gellei50@t-online.hu
No regular opening hours – visits should be pre-booked by email
Bus: 9 – Báthory utca/Bajcsy-Zsilinszky út; Trolley Bus: 70, 72, 73, 78 –
Báthory utca/Bajcsy-Zsilinszky út

In the heart of Budapest, this unique museum is hosted by barber András Gellei, a member of the Gellei dynasty of hairdressers and barbers.

In addition to the museum, the place houses a barber salon and a small shop, which means it is also a great place to have your hair cut.

Artefacts in this collection were originally gathered by hairdresser Károly Pinke and increased later by Gyula Korom, who has been visiting markets and salons since 1996, swelling the collection to several thousand items.

While Europe has seven similarly themed collections, this is the most holistic and is more hands-on in its approach. The exhibition showcases the history of this age-old profession – which included barber-surgeons – and many items can be handled: From early cut-throat razors, right through to modern blades (invented by Gillette), brushes, scissors, hairdryers and travel sets.

The oldest item in the collection is a razor from between the 16th and 17th centuries, restored by the National Museum. The largest pieces are the furniture and old barber chairs, some from as far away as the US.

In the past, the tasks of the barber–surgeon were many and varied. Aside from simple grooming, he was also required to perform venesection (blood-letting) and tooth extraction. Tools for these are also displayed in the glass cabinets. Barber shops also traditionally functioned as men's clubs, which were places to exchange ideas in a unique atmosphere.

THE PAINTING
AT 28 TERÉZ KÖRÚT

Part of the scenery for a production at the Opera House

1066 Budapest, 28 Teréz körút
Private property
Can sometimes be seen if you ask politely
Metro: M1 – Oktogon

From the outside, it is hard to believe that the unassuming house at 28 Teréz körút contains a small secret gem: Above the rectangular stairway, attached to the ceiling, is a large and beautiful painted canvas. The view from the ground floor, from the centre of the stairway is particularly stunning. Little is known about the painting except that it was originally part of the scenery for a production at the Opera House.

Designed by architect Alajos Augenfeld, the house was built by cattle trader Antal Löwy in 1898. Its most noteworthy inhabitants were architects Marcell Komor and Dezső Jakab. At the beginning of the 20th century, the Ullmann sisters' fashion store occupied the ground floor.

NEARBY

Skála Kópé mini statue

In the area in front of the glass-clad building of Skála Metró department store, close to the stairs leading to the underground area, a tiny statue can be spotted. It is one of the artworks of Mihály Kolodko (see p. 28). The figure depicts Skála Kópé – a mascot for the department store network called Skála Coop. It is riding on a receipt with a bar code for a reason: The introduction of the bar code system by Skála was a big novelty in Hungary in the 1980s. The red heart on the guy's chest refers to the old slogan: 'A szívem a vásárlóké' – 'My heart belongs to customers'.

THE HUNGARIAN UNIVERSITY OF FINE ARTS

A masterpiece of Neo-Renaissance architecture

1062 Budapest, 69 Andrássy út
Visit during the European Heritage Days in September or during organised
events: see mke.hu/english/ for details
Metro: M1 – Vörösmarty utca

Housed in a beautiful Neo-Renaissance palace on Andrássy út, the Hungarian University of Fine Arts features a splendid interior that can be visited during the European Heritage Days in September or during events organised by the university (see opposite).

From the entrance (freely accessible), the richly decorated upper foyer can be seen, supported by doric columns, while the ceiling is decorated with historicist decorative painting and a replica statue of the famous *Apollo Belvedere*. The main staircase that leads to the upper level was placed on the side of the foyer. It is covered by an egg-shaped dome featuring allegorical paintings by the renowned master, Károly Lotz, symbolising painting, sculpture, architecture, drawing, copper casting, applied arts and art history.

On the upper level, a splendid corridor leads to the rooms of the university's directorate. The stained glass windows were created by the greatest master of the time, Miksa Róth. The four paintings on the ceiling are symbolic depictions of harmony, beauty, reality and imagination.

A copy of the Bevilacqua palace in Verona

The building was inspired by the Italian Renaissance style: Its main facade was inspired by the Bevilacqua palace in Verona.

© Attila Lerbocs

© Lo Scaligero

The building was built between 1875 and 1877 by architect Adolf Lang for the National Society of Fine Arts (Magyar Képzőművészeti Társulat). Founded in 1861 in order to promote arts in Hungary, the society grew from 154 members to more than 7,000 by 1896. Today, the Műcsarnok (Arts Hall) can be visited in Heroes' Square.

A secret heaven of cinema nostalgia

Facultas Secondary Grammar School
1078 Budapest, 46 Hernád utca (4th floor)
+36 (1) 618 4133 – hernadhaz.hu – pestimozi@eromuvhaz.hu
Prior booking required – open on weekdays only
Trolleybus: 74 – Nefejelcs utca, 78 – Bethlen Gábor tér

On the top floor of the Facultas Secondary Grammar School, two rooms that used to be classrooms have been home to a secret collection of cinematic ephemera since 2020: memorabilia saved from former cinemas in the city ranging from seats, to pieces of furniture, to old projectors. As the building is owned by the 7th district municipality of Budapest, the collection, which is owned by the Budapest Cinema History Foundation, focuses on the cinemas in this area of the city.

One hall, titled 'cinemas of Pest', is furnished like an old cinema with original film posters, photographs of famous actors and even a small buffet desk. A small cubicle in the corner is the cashier's office, with original signs such as '18+ only', 'wide screen film', and the seating chart for the Felszabadulás Cinema. (The word *felszabadulás* refers to the liberation of Hungary from Nazi occupation by the Red Army in 1944–45.)

The screening hall is equipped with seats saved from several cinemas (Apolló, Puskin, Alkotmány and Jókai), accompanied by a large black box: a loudspeaker that used to operate behind the screen of the Európa Cinema. The last section is located behind the seats, where there is a large SK102/B type film projection machine – a Hungarian model produced in 1966 – which used to operate in the town of Hódmezővásárhely in

an outdoor cinema. Following renovation work, it is now perfectly functional. The same type of machine was used in Budapest in the Csillag Cinema. Next to the projector, film storage cabinets and a large xenon bulb can be seen.

The other hall features a small exhibition with posters about the history of the cinemas that were once in the 7th district of Budapest. This room is also used for events: There are regular programmes such as guided tours, photography and film workshops, and events about Hungarian films, photography and cinemas, for example .

Cinemas in Budapest – from Lumière to Multiplexes

Cinema arrived for the first time in Budapest on 10 May 1896, when films made by the French Lumière brothers were presented in the coffee house of the Hotel Royal. While in Budapest, the Lumière's team also shot a short film about the millennial parade in the Castle District, celebrating 1,000 years of Hungarian history. In the same year, the first cinema, the Ikonográf, was opened, although most screenings still took place in tents, coffee houses or amusement parks. The cinema with the longest lifespan started in 1899 with projections in Velence Café. As the projector was manually operated, the owner needed someone who could rotate the handle at a steady speed to roll the film. The café was converted to a proper cinema in 1918, and finally closed in 1995 after 96 years of activity. The first permanent cinema building was that of *Projectograph*, opened in 1899 in Erzsébet körút, followed by *Apolló* on the plot where the building of the Corvin Department Store stands today in Blaha Lujza tér. *Apolló* was the first building to be erected specifically for this function. After that, the number of cinemas rose exponentially: by 1913, there were 111. As a result of the 1918 Spanish flu epidemic, open-air cinemas appeared. In 1922, the first 'multiplex' cinema palace opened: Corvin is still in operation today. The silent film era finished at the end of the 1920s and cinema architecture changed, too: *Simplon* and *Átrium* were built in the modern stlye of the era. On 3 February 1945, when Buda was still under siege, *Uránia* cinema was the first to start screenings again. The cinema, which still exists, features splendid interiors with an oriental atmosphere. It used to be a cabaret: The glass mirrors on the side walls of the main screening hall are a memento of this era. Although television broadcasting started in 1957, Hungarian television had only one channel until 1973 and there was no broadcast on Mondays until the late 80s. That's why the following decades still saw the opening of new cinemas such as *Kőbánya* (1964), *Pest-Buda* (1973) and *Budafok* (1974) – located in the newly built estates of the outer districts. The slowly increasing rate of television ownership, followed by the increasing popularity of home video and colour TV sets led to a fall in cinema audience numbers. In 1990 there were only 75 cinemas left. With the end of the socialist era, privatisation started, but soon led to even more closures. Newly formed civic organisations tried to save a few old cinemas, but most visitors were more attracted by the multiplex cinemas of the shiny new shopping centres. Today, multiplex cinemas can be found in 13 shopping centres and there are 10 arthouse cinemas, struggling to survive.

THE DRAGON OF
THE PEKÁRY HOUSE

Where a statue meets a great storyteller

1077 Budapest, 47 Király utca
Trolley Bus: 70, 78 – Akácfa utca

On the corner of Nagymező utca and Király utca stands an old house with a faithfully restored Neo-Gothic façade. Up above one of the corner balconies, perhaps protecting the house from intruders, is a dragon with outstretched wings.

The house was built in 1847 by Ferenc Brein for city police chief Imre Pekáry, hence the name of the house. It was also home to the popular journalist and writer Gyula Krúdy, who lived here from 1899 to 1901, though it is not known in which apartment. By the 1870s, as a consequence of the soft stone used for the carvings on the building, many of the decorations were sadly deteriorating. This is most likely the reason why the dragon's head fell off. However, Krúdy had another idea: According to his novel *Seven Owls*, the balcony was where a female author regularly accepted guests and conducted liaisons with her 'fancy men'. Following a visit from the publisher Gyula Déri, the head of the dragon fell onto the balcony. Maybe the dragon could not take the bluster? The house was restored in several phases from 2010, including a restoration of the dragon.

THE CRYPT
OF ST. STEPHEN BASILICA

A memorial to the glorious days of Hungarian football

1051 Budapest, 1 Szent István tér
Sunday 8am
Metro: M1, M2, M3 – Deák tér

While the Basilica is a tourist hotspot, its crypt is hardly known by tourists or even locals. Built in the first phase of the construction of the Basilica in classicist style, the grandiose interior houses as well as the grave of one of the most famous Hungarians, football player Ferenc Puskás, among other members of the famous 'Golden Team'.

Puskás was the most famous member of the world famous Hungarian Golden Team, and later played for Real Madrid. He was buried here in 2006 and was followed by three fellow players: Sándor Kocsis died in 1979 and was reburied in the crypt in 2012; in 2014, Gyula Grosics; and in 2015, Jenő Buzánszky, the last surviving member of the Golden Team. The crypt could be considered a shrine for football fans.

However, it is not open to the general public: Only family members of those buried here are permitted. But there is a 30-minute morning ceremony on weekdays at 8:00am held in the crypt in Hungarian.

Visitors to the crypt are impressed by the spacious interior and rows of thick white columns. Circular chapels in the corners look onto the central pillars and main supporting walls, while the vaults of the nave and the transept are supported by dual rows of more robust columns, which in turn support the enormous weight of the dome above.

The path to the Basilica's construction (with the initial aim to replace a smaller church that stood here) was not a smooth one. The collection of money for the construction began in the 1810s, but construction did not start until 1851 with the architect Jozsef Hild, a well-known follower of classicism. However, Hild died in 1867, and soon after his death, the large central dome collapsed due to the weakness of the bricks used to support the arches.

Construction continued under the leadership of Miklós Ybl, architect of the Castle Garden and the Opera House. Ybl redesigned the building, but the crypt was already built by then – hence the difference in style between the Neo-Renaissance church and the classicism of the crypt. Alas, even Ybl couldn't finish the construction. Following his death, the interior decorations were finished under the supervision of József Kauser, and it was finally completed in 1905.

In 1947 'worker's negligence' during restoration caused a fire and the dome burned down, but with the help of government aid and collected funds it was soon restored to its former glory.

THE MICHAEL JACKSON TREE   ⑮

A historic site for Michael Jackson fans

1051 Budapest, Erzsébet tér (by Hotel Kempinski)
Metro: M1, M2, M3 – Deák Ferenc tér

In 1994 Michael Jackson came to Budapest to shoot a promo video for his 'HIStory' album. He visited twice more in 1996: once to check out the People's Stadium (now replaced by the Puskás Arena), and once to play a concert in the stadium. While in the city, the King of Pop stayed in the Corvinus Royal Suite of the Kempinski Hotel, and his fans still remember the time. On a corner of Erzsébet tér, overlooked by the Kempinski Hotel, there is a tree with lots of photos attached to its trunk. This was the spot where fans greeted their idol. When Jackson died in 2009, fans once again gathered around this spot and began attaching mementoes to the tree. Many fans still visit the tree twice in a year: on his birthday on 29 August, and on 25 June, the anniversary of his death.

> The hotel also preserved its guestbook containing Michael Jackson's signature.

NEARBY

Mr Bean's Teddy Bear mini statue

On the wall of the large historic building at 6 Harmincad utca, a mini statue can be spotted right by the main entrance. The tiny artwork is by Mihály Kolodko (see p. 28), and shows a teddy bear. Its resemblence with the stuffed animal of Mr. Bean is no coincidence – the building used to be home to the embassy of the United Kingdom.

PORTUGUESE POEMS UNDER DEÁK TÉR

Ceramic tile artwork with a secret message

1075 Budapest, Deák Ferenc tér
Metro: M1, M2, M3 – Deák tér

Each tile on the walls of Deák tér station on the M3 line has a single letter painted on it. While decorative, it also has a hidden message.

In 1996 Hungary celebrated the 1000th anniversary of the settlement of Hungarian ancestors in the Carpathian Basin. As part of this event, the metro company of Lisbon, *Metropolitano de Lisboa*, offered this tiled wall to BKV, the public transport company of Budapest. The tiles were created by the Portuguese painter Joao Vieira (born 1934) and were produced at the Fábrica Cerámica Viúva Lamego. The artwork was inaugurated on 19 August 1996.

On one side you will find excerpts of Hungarian poems. The authors' names appear in 2x2 tile-sized letters: ADY (Endre Ady), JOZSEF (Attila József) and PETOFI (Sándor Petőfi). The poems appear in the following order from left to right:
- Sándor Petőfi (1823–1849): *Szabadság, Szerelem* – Freedom and Love (Liberdade, Amor)

- Sándor Petőfi: *A nép nevében* – In the Name of the People (Em nome do Povo)
- Endre Ady (1877–1919): *Elillant évek szőlőhegyén* – On Vine Hills of Years Gone By (Na vinha dos anos fanados)
- Sándor Petőfi: *Az Álom* – The Dream (O Sonho)
- József Attila (1905–1937): *A Dunánál* – By the Danube (No Danúbio)

On the other side are Hungarian translations of Portuguese poems. The larger letters refer to PESSOA, CÉSARO* and CAMOES. The poems appear in the following order from left to right:

- Pessoa (Álvaro de Campos) (1888–1935): *Opiárium* – Opiary (Opiário)
- Luís de Camões (1524 – 1580): *Mit akartok, örök vágyakozások?* – What do you want of me, endless regret? (Que me quereis, perpétuas saudades)
- Cesário Verde (1855–1886): *Bezárt éj* – Dark Night (Noite Fechada)
- Pessoa: *Ő, az az aratómunkásnő énekel* – She sings, poor reaper (Ela canta, pobre ceifeira)
- Luís de Camões: *Hibáim, balsors, lobogó szerelmem* – My errors, ill fortune, and ardent love (Erros meus, má fortuna, amor ardente)

Although most Hungarians don't speak a word of Portuguese, the first word ('Opiárium') is easily recognised, giving rise to an urban legend claiming that there are secret drugs-related messages hidden in the tiles. It is not true.

* The name on the tiles was misspelled: Cesário is the correct spelling.

THE RELIEF OF A WILD MAN ⑱

Historical advertisements

1075 Budapest, 5 Károly körút
Metro: M2 – Astoria; Tram: 47, 49 – Astoria; Bus: 5, 7, 8E, 9, 108E, 110, 112, 133E – Astoria

On Károly körút, house number 5 offers two unique features, if you take a look at its façade carefully. In contrast with its modern façade, the building features an old relief and a turret on its top. The story began in 1680 in Dresden, Germany, when Philipp Strobel opened an inn and a guest house under the name 'Wilder Mann' (wild man). The business was inherited by Lüder Hildebrand in 1702, and then by his daugher Henriette and her husband. Within the same year, the couple sold the business to a group of four businessmen, led by Johann Georg Jobst who opened a network of Wilder Mann inns all over Europe, including Frankfurt, Prague, Salzburg, Vienna and in Cegléd, Pécs and Pest in Hungary. Opened in 1736 at the corner of Károly körút and Dob utca, the Budapest unit did not prove to be very successful: In 1744, it was replaced by a convenience store, dedicated to the wild man (Zum Wilder Mann). That's

when Lőrinc Dunaiszky sculpted a large relief which was placed on the façade of the building as an advertisement for the business. The building burnt down in 1807 but was rebuilt and the relief was saved. The most famous business of the building was the 'Diana' pharmacy, opened in 1898 (and later moved to a new address) and famous for the Diana-branded salt peas product. In the following decades, the building changed ownership many times until its demolition in 1929.

The wild man relief was saved again and placed on the façade of the new building as a memento of the former inn. When the new building was designed, its owners asked to build a tower on the corner of the building shaped like the bottle of the Diana salt peas. but the authorities did not approve this idea. As a compromise, a tower looking somewhat like the bottle's cap was given permission.

At the end of the Second World War, as well as during the 1956 Revolution, it was used for shooting at the enemy. Today it belongs to the flat beneath.

> The house is often referred to as the Marczibányi House as one of its owners, from 1820, was János.

THE NEON LIGHTS OF THE MUSEUM OF ELECTRICAL ENGINEERING

Each neon sign promoted an old socialist company

1075 Budapest, 21 Kazinczy utca
kozlekedesimuzeum.hu
Wed–Sat 10am–4pm
Trolley bus: 74 – Károly körút (Astoria M); or a short walk from M1, M2, M3 – Deák tér

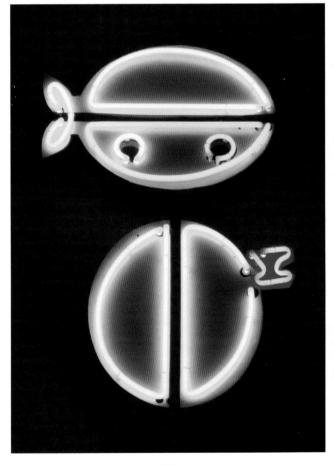

In socialist Hungary, a government programme encouraged the proliferation of colourful neon lights in the capital's high-traffic areas. Once characteristic features of Budapest by night, after 1990 the lights began to disappear, however, together with the old socialist companies that they promoted. But some were saved and can still be seen, hidden in the courtyard of the Museum of Electrical Engineering.

The lights were rescued by 'neon saver' community groups, and at least a dozen of them now illuminate the night in this hidden corner of the party district of Budapest. They also serve as a reminder of the old socialist companies of Hungary: the white dove figure of the Patyolat dry cleaner, the basket of the Csemege supermarket chain, the winking owl of a second-hand bookshop, the coffee bean figure of the Omnia brand …

The Bauhaus-style transformer station, now a museum, was built in Erzsébetváros in 1934 and designed by architects Ágost Gerstenberger and Károly Arvé. The building behind it is even older: It was built in 1893 as a machine hall, where the 30kV electricity of the Kelenföld Power Station was transformed to 10kV (see p. 200). During the 1960s, the main network was upgraded and the machinery in the building became outdated – the new 120kV building is the larger, red brick building in nearby Dob utca.

The museum took over the building, opening in 1975. Its exhibition rooms are named after Hungarian inventors and relate to various aspects of electricity: lighting technology, household appliances and medical instruments, the electrification of the railways, the history of the Ganz factory, the story of the flow meter and the production of electricity. In 2006 the exhibition was completely reworked to make it more interactive. Today's visitors can drive a tram, generate high voltage with a treadmill, play with vacuum tubes and then marvel at the 'Neon Parade' exhibition.

The lights are not switched on every day, so it is best to visit during the Night of Museums, the Month of Architecture, or Design Week. The museum does, however, plan to turn the lights on more often in the future.

A LOTZ FRESCO
ON BLAHA LUJZA TÉR

Look up!

1088 Budapest, Blaha Lujza tér
Metro: M2 – Blaha Lujza tér

Blaha Lujza Square, where the Nagykörút ring road intersects the busy Rákóczi út, is among the busiest junctions of Budapest. It is characterised by high volumes of traffic, crowded buses, trams and metros, and an underpass with several exits. But take exit D from the rather ugly underpass and when you get to the top of the stairs, stop for a moment and look up. On the ceiling is a fresco by Károly Lotz, the most famous creator of wall art in Budapest.

The house itself – called the László House – was built by Zsigmond László in 1893–1897 following a design by the architect István Kiss.

A lawyer by profession, Zsigmond László (1845–1920) probably knew the architect through his job: Kiss designed several judicial buildings. The fresco by the entrance door depicts various female figures, allegedly modelled on Lotz's daughter Kornélia. The fresco was restored in 1978.

Károly Lotz (1833–1904) was a German-born painter whose early works were romantic landscapes. He later created large murals and frescoes in Budapest and elsewhere. In 1882 he was made a professor at several art academies in Budapest. Following his death, his paintings, sketches and drawings were donated to the state and are now in the Museum of Fine Arts. His most famous works in Budapest include the ceiling of the Opera and murals in the Hungarian Academy of Sciences, the Parliament building, the National Museum, Vigadó, the Basilica and in Keleti (Eastern) railway station. His grave can be found in the Kerepesi út cemetery.

The main pharmacist at the corner pharmacy was Hugó Örkény, the father of the famous Hungarian writer István Örkény, author of *One Minute Stories*.

THE CERAMICS
OF ÁRKÁD BAZÁR

Where the largest toy store in Budapest once stood

1074 Budapest, 22 Dohány utca
Bus: 5, 7, 8E, 108E, 110, 112, 133E, 178 – Uránia

The house at the corner of Dohány utca and Síp utca boasts beautiful ceramic tile decorations that are often overlooked. They used to promote the largest toy store in the city in the early 20th century. Above the main gate is the name of the former store, Árkád Bazár: Késmárky and Illés's Toy Store. Above, two children with wooden swords and folded paper hats are playing soldiers on either side of a small monkey riding a rocking horse. The façades are clad in white ceramics, with decorative motifs based on Hungarian folk art inspired by Viennese Art Nouveau, especially the works of Otto Wagner.

The building was erected in 1909 by Késmárky and Illés – the company had enjoyed several decades in business with a high reputation, successfully operating a store in the most popular bathing town in the world, Karlsbad.

The lower levels of Árkád Bazár were taken up by the most fantastic toy store of its time. The ground floor had arcades on both sides, with the main entrance at the corner. Stepping inside was like heaven for an early 20th-century child. Dolls dressed in clothes from around the globe, sledges, electric model railways, model ships and rocking horses were stocked in the hundreds. The range was unprecedented in Budapest, offering fun to everyone from workers to aristocrats.

As most of the goods were produced in Hegybánya, the Treaty of Trianon peace agreement of 1920 meant the loss of its most important supplier of toys, leading to financial losses and finally the closure of the business in 1924. But a second period of prosperity came in 1960–1969 when the place was home to Metró Klub. The club was set up for the builders of the metro, and also inspired the name of a band (Metró) that played here. It was famous as the centre of Hungarian beat music and had capacity crowds for many years. In the following decades, the place changed ownership and function several times, but the Metró Klub neon sign remained on the façade until 2010.

If access through the gate on the Dohány utca side is possible, there are more ceramic decorations to be seen. It is a private property. Please ask politely if it is possible to see them.

22

THE FORGOTTEN METALLIC STRUCTURE OF THE FORMER NATIONAL CASINO

A surviving memory of the socialist era

1053 Budapest, 20 Kossuth Lajos utca
Metro: M2 – Astoria

Built in 1896, the large building known today as the House of Hungarians at the corner of Semmelweis utca and Kossuth Lajos utca has a metal structure on the top reminiscent of the Kremlin. For a short while after 1919, the building was taken over by the communists. They eventually left and the building became a casino. This closed down after the Second World War and two institutions moved in: the Hungarian-Soviet Friendship Association and the House of Soviet Science and Culture.

When the trend for neon advertising hit the city, a red neon Kremlin was placed on top of the building. After 1990, the building was occupied by the World Federation of Hungarians, but the structure that held the neon lighting was never removed and is still visible from the end of Magyar utca.

23

THE WOODEN PAVING BLOCKS OF UNGER HOUSE

Helping horses and carriages make less noise …

1053 Budapest, 7 Múzeum körút
Open weekdays only
Metro: M2 – Astoria

Designed by architect Miklós Ybl in 1852, the house at 7 Múzeum körút was commissioned by Henrik Unger, hence its name. There are a few small shops within the building, so getting to the inner yard (from either Múzeum körút or Magyar utca) is quite easy during the day.

In addition to a fine example of romantic architecture, you will be able to see a fantastic small detail: one of the last examples of a wooden road surface in Budapest. In comparison to traditional stone pavement, wooden paving blocks were preferred by the elite, as horses and carriages made less noise on that surface than on any kind of stone. The whole ground and gateways were covered with wooden blocks. Only the inner yard was resurfaced with stone in the 1960s.

In addition to this, the house impresses with its rich decorations combining Byzantine, Gothic, Renaissance, and Arabesque elements. The first floor boasts seven balconies, supported by griffins. The gateway, stairway and windows of the inner yard are also noteworthy, despite the poor condition of the house (it was last renovated in the 1950s and 1960s).

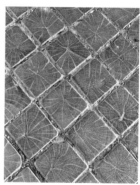

The Unger family made a fortune from smith work and iron trading, based at a workshop on this site. When the head of the family died in 1847, the workshop was inherited by four children, but they made an agreement to leave this piece of heritage exclusively to one son, Henrik.

Henrik quit the family business and made his living in property. By the mid-1870s, he was the fifth largest taxpayer in the city.

Other original wooden block surfaces in Budapest

In 1871 Clark Ádám tér and the Chain Bridge were paved with wood, although it was soon apparent the humid environment was detrimental to the material.

When it opened in 1876, Andrássy út was covered with pine wood blocks. However, the road was resurfaced with new, impregnated wood elements in 1884, the last remains of which were removed in 1960. Originally, József Attila utca, and Margit Bridge were also surfaced with wooden blocks.

Today, only a few areas still have their original wooden block surface:
The Óbuda Museum in the Zichy palace
The courtyard of 3 Petőfi Sándor utca / 4 Városház utca
The Petőfi Museum of Literature
Apartment houses at 15 Erkel utca and 13 Tárnok utca
The Batthyány palace at 3 Dísz tér.

THE CLOCK AT ELTE UNIVERSITY CAMPUS

A super accurate clock, controlled by another clock inside the building via electromagnetic contact

1088 Budapest, 4 Múzeum körút
Metro: M2 – Astoria

Considered the most reliable clock in the city, since 1888 a clock has stood in front of the ELTE university campus. Originally proposed by Alajos Schuller, the first clock to stand here was produced in Vienna. This was replaced in 1913 by a precision grandfather clock, produced by Viktor Hoser, a watchmaker who worked in Apród utca. The Hoser family had a long tradition in watchmaking: An ancestor, János Mihály, supplied the court of Vienna during Maria Theresa's reign. Viktor Hoser also supplied Svábhegyi Observatory with precision mechanisms.

The clock on Múzeum körút is controlled by another clock inside the building via electromagnetic contact. This control clock was set using astronomical time data every second or third week, supplied by the Institute of Cosmography. The institute also supplied the exact time to Parliament, the state railways, ministries, and many other institutions on the telephone network. Thanks to this astronomical control, Central European Time could be displayed with 0.1-second accuracy. When the data could be transmitted via radio, the accuracy improved to 0.01 seconds.

> During repairs in 1926, the connection between the two clocks had to be cut for a few days. The general public was informed that the clock might be less accurate for a short while, with a difference of up to five seconds. In reality it was less than three seconds.

NEARBY

Franz Joseph mini statue ㉕
Balustrade of the green Szabadság (Liberty) bridge, close to Fővám tér

The bridge was originally named after the famous emperor of the Austrian–Hungarian monarchy. He is depicted sitting in a hammock, and many of them appeared on the bridge when it was closed for several weeks and the usual traffic was replaced by relaxing university students. The little statue is attached to the railing with two padlocks.

PLATE IN MEMORY OF THE GREAT FLOOD OF 1838

A reminder of devastation

1 Bródy Sándor utca, corner of Bródy Sándor utca and Múzeum körút
M3, M4 – Kálvin tér

Along the garden of the Hungarian National Museum in Bródy Sándor utca, the green iron fence has a red marble plate where a hand points at a line. It was the highest water lever there on 15 March 1838, when a flood destroyed much of the inner city. The word 'árvíz', also seen on the plate, is Hungarian for flood.

It was the early spring of 1838. The lower part of the Danube was still frozen, but above it had begun to melt, creating drift ice. The large pieces created blockages, causing water levels to rise. The water eventually broke through the dams on the northern side of Pest on 13 March, flooding the area known today as Nagykörút. Early the next day, another blockage formed above Csepel Island, the water level in Pest rose again and more dams were breached by the icy Danube. The highest water levels in the city were measured on 15 March, peaking at between 9 and 10 metres. Much of the city was devastated.

During the flood, Earl Miklós Wesselényi became a hero. He gathered people and took boats to rescue others and save lives as buildings

collapsed. His bravery is commemorated on the side of the church in Ferenciek tere.

Only a few areas remained dry: Deák tér, Nyugati tér, Kossuth tér and Ferenciek tere. A little chapel at the end of Kőmíves utca also escaped the devastation. It was located roughly at the end of what is now Andrássy út, making it the perfect place to build the basilica.

After the flood, two competing ideas emerged: to fill up the flooded areas, or to regulate the Danube with new dams. Until 1870, the first idea prevailed, and water levels were indicated on many building walls.

Other reminders of the 1838 flood

Dotted around the city, dozens of stone plates are reminders of the 1838 flood, the most devastating in Budapest's history. Here are a few:

– 27 Rákóczi út: The small Rókus chapel stands closer to the road than neighbouring buildings. The entrance gate is a few steps lower than the road surface, as a reminder of the formerly lower road level. By the entrance gate, the stone plate with an arrow sign can be found easily

– 23 Szerb utca: Placed there in 1938, on the 100th anniversary, this memorial features a map of the flooded area. This is a replica, as the original stone plate belongs to the Budapest History Museum

– 15 Döbrentei utca: This plate includes text in Hungarian and in Serbian, as there used to be a large Serbian community living in the area. Another plate on this old house commemorates the flood in 1775

– 4 Szerb utca: The plate is in Serbian, as it is on the wall of a Serbian Orthodox Church. The water mark there is 270 cm above the current floor level (Note the date: According to the calendar used by the Orthodox Church, 3 March corresponded to 15 March. Therefore, the date on the plate is correct)

– 5 Salétrom utca: This sign was written in German and can be found under the gateway that leads to the Protestant church (the use of German was quite common in Hungary in the era)

– 7 Apáczay Csere János utca: This red marble plaque is in German too

– Horváth Mihály tér: The stone plate can be found above the holy water basin. The horizontal line is 156 cm above the floor level

– 41 Rákóczi út: This is probably the newest of them all. It was placed there in 1988, on the 150th anniversary of the flood, by the Middle Danube Valley Water Directorate

ANDRÁSSY UNIVERSITY (FESTETICS PALACE)

㉗

Ballrooms and salons in the 'Magnates' Quarter'

1088 Budapest, 3 Pollack Mihály tér
festeticspalota.hu
Open only during Cultural Heritage Days in September and for private events
Metro: M3, M4 – Kálvin tér

Open only during Cultural Heritage Days on the third weekend of September, or if you are lucky enough to be invited to a private event, the Festetics Palace is well worth a visit, especially for its neoclassical staircase and its four majestic halls inspired by the Italian Renaissance.

The palace was commissioned by György Festetics, to be designed by Miklós Ybl, the architect of the Castle Garden and the Opera House. Construction began in 1745 and lasted more than a century.

The Mirror Hall, as its name suggests, is characterised by large mirrors on the walls, enhanced by the maple and oak parquet under foot.

The chandelier in the centre of the hall is the only original piece, the others being replicas made by the same manufacturer. In the equally aptly named Marble Hall, which served as a salon for receiving guests, Ybl used a fanlight structure, allowing abundant sunlight to stream in.

The Andrássy Hall was the music salon when the Festetics family lived here, as indicated by the theme of the smaller paintings on the walls. Finally, the Festetics Hall was once the dining area.

This room suffered the most damage during the 1956 revolution, and today functions as an event space, alongside the other halls. (There was originally a direct way down to the basement, where the kitchen and adjacent rooms were located.)

The building was nationalised in 1933 and was home to several institutions in the following decades. In 1989 it was the site of negotiations between new parties and the old socialist leaders, leading to the first free elections and a change of political regime.

The palace was restored in the early 2000s, and has been home to the newly established Andrássy Gyula German Speaking University of Budapest since 2003.

THE CHIMNEY SWEEP HOUSE (28)

An old statue for an old profession

1088 Budapest, 15 Bródy Sándor utca
M4 – Rákóczi tér

On the first floor of the facade of 15 Bródy Sándor utca, a strange but beautiful statue shows a man holding a ladder in his right arm and a kind of brush in his left hand. His black uniform, which covers him up to the head, is that of a chimney sweep.

The owner of the building was indeed Mihály Devecis (Del Vecchio), a chimney sweep entrepreneur of Italian origin, who asked Károly Hild to design the building in classicist style in 1851–55, following the opening of the nearby National Museum in 1847.

Placed there around 1855 probably as publicity, the statue was renovated in 2023.

THE KÁROLYI-CSEKONICS PALACE

Dracula's staircase

1088 Budapest, 17 Múzeum utca
portal.kre.hu/
Open during events only
Metro: M3, M4 – Kálvin tér

Designed by the famous architectural firm Fellner and Helmer (who also designed the Comedy Theatre and the Operetta and Musical Theatre), the Neo-Baroque palace at number 17 Múzeum utca boasts a stunning main hall featuring wooden carvings and a spectacular wooden staircase. Built in 1881 by Margit Csekonics, the wife of István Károlyi, a member of the wealthy Károlyi family, it can be visited during events.

A hub of aristocratic society, home to extravagant balls and social events, the palace was enlarged in 1890: A new floor was added, along with the staircase that is the real gem of the palace. Carved in the workshop of Endre Thék, the oak stairs lead to the first floor and the 300-capacity ballroom.

At the top is the griffin crest of the Károlyi family, while the railings are decorated with floral motifs and animal figures.

Following István Károlyi's death, the building became home to the French Embassy, then the Swedish Embassy, a trade society named the Baross Association, and the Lenin Institute. In 1955 the National Technical Library moved in, and two additional floors were built on the Reviczky utca side.

This part of the complex was later used by the Farkas Kempelen Student Information Centre, before being taken over by an institution belonging to the Ministry of Justice.

Following renovation in 2021, the Károli Gáspár Reformed University has become the newest resident.

Despite the relatively small scale, the rich decorations exude the style of a true aristocratic dwelling. Windows feature simpler adornments on the ground floor and richer ones on the first. Small balconies on the first floor have Baroque shell-shaped decorations on their parapets. The symmetrical façade is decorated with Baroque elements on the Múzeum utca side.

The Reviczky utca side is simpler: It was originally the entrance for horse-drawn carriages, and included the servants' rooms and other service areas.

The building was used as a location for the 2003 vampire film *Underground*, and the 2007 film *Eichmann*.

THE STAIRCASE
OF THE WENCKHEIM PALACE

Elves on the stairway and beautiful interiors

Metropolitan Library
1088 Budapest, 1 Szabó Ervin tér
+36 (1) 411-5019
csoportvezetes@fszek.hu
Guided tours available for groups of 10-20 (call or email) / visitor ticket
available for individual visits
Mon–Fri 10am–8pm, Saturday 10am–4pm (closed in July)
Staircase visible only during only during open days (see fszek.hu for the dates)
Metro: M3, M4 – Kálvin tér

W hile the beautiful Wenckheim Palace that gives home to the Ervin Szabó Municipal Library is popular among visitors, the main staircase and adjacent rooms remain hidden to most of them, as they are not open to the public and can be seen only during open days.

In the main stairway that is opened to visitors only during open days,

stunning marble treads lead from the entrance hall to the mezzanine, supported by four intricately carved columns beneath the vaulted ceiling. The lower flight features ornate chandeliers and marble putti, while the main columns are supported by four elves.

A large skylight above the landing allows natural light to flood the room, beautifully picking out the Rococo decorations.

From the landing, the flights turn back on themselves before meeting the balcony at the top.

The building is topped by the Wenckheim coat-of-arms and a nine-point crown, the pinnacle of a richly-decorated façade that suitably reflects the magnificent interior.

Count Frigyes Wenckheim (1842-1912) was a well-known aristocrat and Member of Parliament.

At the end of the 1880s, Arthur Meinig was entrusted with the task of building the palace. It incorporates elements of Neo-Renaissance and Baroque. Following the death of the count, the palace changed ownership and functions several times until it was eventually purchased by the City Council on behalf of the Metropolitan Library. Opened in 1931, it was named after social scientist and librarian Ervin Szabó in 1946.

Further historic rooms of the palace can be visited with a visitor ticket, allowing entrance without the possibility to request items from the storage rooms and without the right to lend books. The most impressive halls are up the stairs in the palace building: the old Saloon with Boudoirs either side, one silver, one gold; the Small Ballroom and the Large Ballroom, with a gallery in between for the orchestra; the Dining Room; and the dark wood-clad Smoking Room.

THE MOSAICS OF
M4 KÁLVIN TÉR STATION

Kodály's underground music

1091 Budapest, Kálvin tér
Metro: M3, M4 – Kálvin tér

The first thing that stands out on arrival at Kálvin tér metro station is the mosaic of colourful tiles on the walls.

While many people of course notice them when they enter the station, few realise what they are: Viewed from the top of the escalators, they clearly appear as musical notes.

The pattern was designed by Katalin Fábry and the notes are from *Psalmus Hungaricus*, a work by the Hungarian composer Zoltán Kodály, who worked out the Kodály Method (do-re-mi … etc. – used by Kodály as part of his programme for musical education).

The music depicted by the tiles was composed on the 50th anniversary of the day that Buda, Óbuda and Pest were united to create Budapest.

A clever reference to the Protestant church on the square above the station

Being a psalm, the music score is also a clever reference to the Protestant church on the square above the station. The notes are from the part of the work that includes the line: *A szegényeket felmagasztalod, a kevélyeket aláhajigálod* – meaning 'You raise the poor, you cast down the disdained'. Perhaps the perfect quote to surround the escalators and elevators of a metro station.

At the junction of the escalators, the pattern in the mosaic forms some of Kodály's handwriting. There is also a Space Invader hidden somewhere on the walls.

REMAINS OF THE OLD CITY WALL ㉜

Mostly demolished or built into houses, but still appearing here and there

Along the inner ring road 'Kiskörút'
Guided tours possible, see Introduction for operators
Tram: 47, 49 – Deák tér to Fővám tér

Just like many other cities, Pest was a walled city in the late Middle Ages. In 1241 the city fell victim to a Mongolian invasion. Today nothing remains of this first wall. Recovery was slow, but during the reign of King Mathias (1458–1490), a new city wall was built. This encompassed a larger area, enabling the growth of Pest from 23 to 55 acres. Built from limestone, the wall had casemates and crenellations on top, and from the 16th century, roundels were added for extra strength. Roughly two metres deep and 8.5 metres tall, it ran straight along the Danube before curving around the city. The curved part ran along today's Károly körút / Astoria / Múzeum körút / Kálvin tér / Vámház körút / Fővám tér – i.e. the inner ring road 'Kiskörút'.

Access to the city was via fortified gates: Váci Gate was at the north end of Váci utca, close to Vörösmarty tér, Hatvani Gate (at today's Astoria), and Kecskeméti Gate at today's Kálvin tér. At the end of the 17th century, another gate was built at the southern end, called *Porta Nova* (New Gate).

However, the wall eventually lost its military importance and became an obstacle to the city's growth. Deconstruction of the walls and gates began at the end of the 18th century: In 1783 the wall was cut through at today's Királyi Pál utca, and in 1794 Kecskeméti Gate was pulled down, followed in 1808 by Hatvani Gate. The remaining sections were reused as the walls of newly constructed houses, leading to the formation of today's Kiskörút ring road.

The Great Northern Roundel (Északi nagy rondella) stood at today's Vigadó tér. It was demolished in 1789 and its stones were bought by tanner János Kemnitzer, who built a house on the plot where the tower stood.

These are the remains and traces of the wall that can still be seen …

The old Váci Gate no longer has any visible walls. However, the road surface in front of 1 and 3 Váci utca is marked with the location of some remains that are now underground. The section of wall from here to the Danube disappeared completely, but some remains of the gate were found during archaeological research in 1985. According to an engraving by Hallart-Wening in 1684, this gate had wooden fortifications, unlike all the others. A plaque on the corner of Váci utca and Türr István utca notes that the gate was demolished in 1789.

Remains of the wall were also discovered in the courtyard of the City Hall (28-30 Károly körút, today Városháza Park), but they were reburied and are no longer visible. More remains can be seen at the back of the empty plot at 21 Semmelweis utca, between 24 Károly körút and 21 Semmelweis utca. Research revealed that the wall was fortified with moats on both sides. Hatvani gate was built here in the 15th century. A century later, a roundel roughly 40 metres in diameter with a wooden structure for cannons was added. The gate was equipped with an iron portcullis, a drawbridge and guards. But by the end of the 18th century, the gate was merely a bottleneck for increasing traffic, so the roundel was demolished and houses were built on both sides of the wall. The tower (the last remaining one) was finally pulled down in 1808 because it blocked the view from Hatvani utca and its narrow passage caused congestion during fairs. In 1963, more than a century and a half later, the remains were found during the construction of metro line M2 and the underpass. Only then was the exact location revealed: The tower and the roundel stood in front of and underneath Hotel Astoria. The same construction unfortunately also led to the destruction of most of the wall remains. Today, only a stone plaque in the underpass commemorates the gate (note the graffiti on the plaque, featuring a few figures swimming in the moat – it is several decades old). Another stone plaque, with a more accurate depiction of the tower, can be found on the wall of 20 Kossuth Lajos utca.

Reconstruction works in the 1940s led to the creation of common inner courtyards for several houses, while uncovering a few remaining sections of the city wall. In the courtyard of 9-11 Múzeum körút, there is a straight section of wall with two pieces of its merlon that were restored in the 1940s – the wall was originally 8.4 metres high and the merlons were 1.35 metres high with a 0.7 metre gap between. The opposite side of this section can be seen in the courtyard of 12 Magyar utca.

On the corner of Ferenczy István utca, a short wall section can be seen in the street. A smaller tower probably stood here. The remains of another were found by archaeologists at 27-29 Múzeum körút. From the staircase of this house, part of the wall can be seen through the first floor window. The wall can also be spotted through the glass of the main gates of 15 Múzeum körút and 29 Múzeum körút, and through a small hole in the main gate of 21 Múzeum körút. The modern buildings at 23-25 and

31-33 have extended backyards, revealing longer wall sections. The most intact pieces can be found in the courtyards of 21 to 33 Múzeum körút. Please note that today these are private properties with limited access.

In 1975, during the construction of metro line M3, the remains of the Kecskeméti gate were discovered. The tower that once stood here was about 6.3 x 6.3 metres, with wall thickness varying from 1.8 to 2.7 metres, its layout and shape probably identical to the other gates. The remains of the roundel were not found. The gate stood until 30 April 1794 and was the second to be demolished after the Váci Gate. A nearby tower was also demolished.

There are two reminders of the old gate in the square: Between the two buildings of Hotel Mercure Korona is a reconstructed piece of wall featuring a replica of a Gothic tombstone from Szakolca, dated 1535. There is also a red marble sculpture in the underpass by Gyula Illés, built in mem-

ory of the Kecskeméti gate of the old city wall and installed in 1983: In the centre, an opening symbolises a gateway to the past, while the artist's cat (Maci) sits nearby. Allegedly, stroking the cat brings you luck.

The last section of the ring road is Vámház körút. On the corner of Bástya utca (numbers 1-11), on a plot that is now a park with a playground, is the largest visible section of the wall. The houses that once stood here were demolished in the 1970s, revealing the remains. Another piece of the wall divides 17-19 Bástya utca from 13/b Királyi Pál utca. On the Bástya utca side, a small section of the ditch in front of the wall can also be seen. Nearby, at 13/b Királyi Pál utca, is a tiny exhibition of the city wall. To enter, visitors must collect a key from the office of Imagine Budapest (18 Királyi Pál utca) on the opposite side of the street. A modest visitor centre showcases the first section of wall that was revealed (in the 1940s), preserved and exhibited to the public. The exhibition is open during office hours – see imaginebp.hu for details.

At the southern end of Váci utca, the darker stones of the road surface and a metal plaque indicate the place where the old city tower and gate might have been. According to the 1684 Hallart-Wening engraving, a semicircular roundel once stood here. In a document dated 1787, city merchants lobbied for its demolition, claiming it was too narrow to cope with the level of traffic. Initially, a passage (*Porta Nova*) was cut into it, and by 1796 it was totally demolished. The large roundel that stood nearby, close to the Danube, was demolished in 1787. Three roundels were originally built along the Danube – none of them remains.

LIBRARY OF THE CENTRAL SEMINARY

A hidden Baroque masterpiece of the Catholic Church

1053 Budapest, 7 Papnövelde utca
Guided tours only, see Introduction for operators – closed in winter
Metro: M3, M4 – Kálvin tér

Constructed between 1760 and 1770, the fabulous library of the Central Seminary (Központi Papnevelő Intézet Könyvtára) was designed by the Pauline monk Antal Rutschman, a member of the Order of Saint Paul, the only Hungarian-founded Catholic order.

Frescoes on the ceiling depict the idea that science and the arts are servants of theology – allegorical figures represent philosophy, medical science, geography, architecture, mathematics, astronomy, literature, poetry and music. At the four corners four saints are depicted: St Ambrose with a beehive; St Augustus with a flaming heart; St Gregory with a dove (the symbol of the Holy Spirit) and St Jerome with a lion.

Initially a small chapel was erected and later replaced by the current church and convent buildings, which were probably built between 1725 and 1742. (Until its demolition in 1720, a mosque had stood on the site.) Due to prolonged works on the interior, the Baroque church was only consecrated in 1776. The building's original Baroque façade was later converted to Neo-Renaissance.

A large crack has appeared on a side wall of the main altar – an unfortunate consequence of the construction of the M3 metro line.

Following the *Abolitio* in 1780 (a regulation imposed by Joseph II dissolving all orders not relating to healing or education), the library books were transferred to the University Library. The monastery building became the headquarters of different state offices – the hall was even used as a casino for some time. In 1803, Count Ferenc Széchenyi brought his own library from Nagycenk and founded the National Museum and the National Library, which opened in this very building, laying the foundations for today's National Széchenyi Library.

Due to the *Abolitio*, ownership of the library hall transferred from church to state. Plans were created to change the ceiling paintings accordingly. In 1803, intending to save the paintings from destruction, the artist attempted to sabotage the ceiling renovation by nailing pieces of cardboard painted with images referencing the Hungarian state. The cardboard has since gone missing. However, during the last renovation (around 1990), restorers discovered the nail marks.

Today's book collection comprises materials from no less than 163 monasteries, mostly from the 16th, 17th and 18th centuries. Fifteen volumes are dated before the year 1500. Only five books are part of the original collection.

A visual trick

A large, dark wooden door welcomes visitors to the second floor. The entrance was intended to be in the centre of the library hall, but the axis was not directly in line with the corridor. The problem was solved using a trick: Only the right side of the door is real; the left cannot be opened.

THE OVEN OF
AN HISTORIC BAKERY

*Memories of an old bakery in the cellar of an
18th-century townhouse*

1056 Budapest, 2 Papnövelde utca
papnovelde2.hu
*Open during the European Heritage Days in September or by prior
arrangement: attila.jeney@gmail.com*
Metro: M3 – Ferenciek tere

In the heart of the city centre, by prior arrangement or during the European Heritage Days in September, it is possible to visit the forgotten remains of an old bakery, complete with its oven, in the labyrinth of the Baroque-era cellar of a classical-style house.

The house is the result of two buildings being combined together in 1841 – they were built by the architect József Hild, a master of Hungarian classical architecture, and had survived the great flood of 1838 (see p. 106). According to old documents, the owner of the original house was Károly Ráth (Carl Rath), the name of a previous mayor of the city. Further research, however, revealed that a master baker had the same name, which is why the sign by the entrance gate bears a correction.

The cellar system of the house is quite meandering, but well worth the struggle to get through. The last room features the brick laid oven. Strangely though, there is no chimney: Maybe it was dismantled during the 1841 construction? Actually, little is known about the past use of the oven. There are no smoke marks on the bricks, and only the size of the oven suggests that a bakery once operated here: Production capacity was sized for commercial sales.

According to a legend, after the 1838 flood many buns remained stuck to the ceiling after being lifted up there by the rising waters.

Opened near Kecskeméti gate (today's Kálvin tér) in 1794, the 'Arany Oroszlán' pharmacy (Golden Lion in Hungarian) moved to the ground floor of this house in 1810. The original fixtures of the pharmacy, dating from the 1830s, can still be seen in the exhibition area of the Kiscelli Museum, having been saved in the early 1950s following the nationalisation of the pharmacy by the communist regime in 1951. For decades, the pharmacy's site was used as a passenger walkway when the street was widened. Today, the site of the pharmacy remains empty, waiting for a new chapter.

RELIEF OF AN ELEPHANT

What is an exotic animal doing in the city centre?

1056 Budapest, 3 Duna utca
Bus: 5, 8E, 108E, 110, 112, 133E, 178

Next to Elisabeth Bridge (*Erzsébet híd*), you have to look up at the top of the corner house at 3 Duna utca in order to see the unusual relief of an elephant.

Built in 1899 by spice merchant Lajos Takáts, thanks to the profits from his store in Kossuth Lajos utca, during the Second World War the house lost its once splendid roof.

The elephant refers to Takáts' coat of arms, which featured a black elephant.

A large portion of the lower floors was rented out in 1908 to Vilmos Zsolnay, the founder of the Zsolnay porcelain factory, which explains the presence of three beautiful ceramic reliefs on the first floor of the façade: On the corner, a fort with five towers symbolises Pécs, the hometown of the factory; on the Váci utca side, men working on a pottery wheel; and on the Duna utca side, women painting ceramics.

UNIVERSITY LIBRARY OF ELTE

A stunning historical library in Budapest

1053 Budapest, 6 Ferenciek tere
Mon–Fri 9am–8pm
Open to visitors with free visitor's card (valid for one year)
The library can also be viewed during the Museums' Night in June or European
Heritage Days in September, or by prior registration for groups, see: konyvtar
elte.hu/en/university-library/library-visit/library-visit-building-tours
Metro: M3 – Ferenciek tere

While the stunning reading room of ELTE University is well-known among university students, very few visitors have in fact heard about it or seen it. It is well worth the effort to admire the beauty of this magnificent 228-square-metre room which is bathed in light, thanks to the glass roof. Frescoes of allegorical figures from the sciences and arts by Károly Lotz watch over the 1.5 million books and other documents that are stored here, including 200 codices and about 77,000 books from the 16th to 18th centuries. The way leading to the room is also decorated with beautiful sgraffiti in the entrance hall and an elegant staircase.

Designed by the architects Antal Szkalnitzky (who also designed the four corner buildings of Oktogon Square) and Henrik Koch Jr, the building was completed in 1876, and was the first one in Budapest to be constructed specifically as a library. Its first and second floors are linked

by a colonnade, topped with a tympanum on the Ferenciek tere side and a small dome at the corner. Within the tympanum, two angels bear the university shield. The grand appearance is further enhanced by Mór Than's sgraffiti depicting mythological figures.

Founded in 1635, ELTE university (Eötvös Lóránd Tudományegyetem / Lóránd Eötvös University of Sciences) is one of the largest and most prestigious public higher education institutions in Hungary. It is associated with five Nobel laureates. The predecessor of Eötvös Loránd University was founded in 1635 by Cardinal Péter Pázmány in Nagyszombat, Kingdom of Hungary (today Trnava, Slovakia) as a Catholic university for teaching theology and philosophy. In 1770, the university was transferred to Buda. It was named Royal University of Pest until 1873, then University of Budapest until 1921, when it was renamed Royal Hungarian Pázmány Péter University after its founder Péter Pázmány.

The Faculty of Science started its autonomous life in 1949 when The Faculty of Theology was separated from the university (now Pázmány Péter Catholic University). The university received its current name in 1950, after one of its most well-known physicists, Baron Loránd Eötvös.

When creating sgraffito art, two or sometimes three coats of plaster, typically in contrasting colours, are layered onto a wall. The upper layer is then scratched through, to reveal the contrasting colour of the lower layer, thereby creating the image.

© LaszloGaramvolgyi

THE RELIEF OF THE MEZ HOUSE

Elaborate artwork hidden in a passage

1052 Budapest, 12 Petőfi Sándor utca / 6 Párizsi utca
Metro: M3 – Ferenciek tere

Many tourists walk through the busy shopping street of Váci utca, unaware that just two corners from there, a passage full of small shops (although many are now empty) is the entrance to number 12 Petőfi Sándor utca.

If you look through the glass door, you will notice that the staircase wall features a large stone relief of weavers at work, created by Ödön Metky, a well-known sculptor of his era.

On the relief there are three women (symbolising spinning, weaving and embroidery) and a younger girl. Designed by architect Gedeon Gerlóczy, the building at the corner of Petőfi Sándor utca and Párizsi utca was built in 1940–43.

The investor was MEZ, a German cotton yarn production company based in Nagyatád, Transylvania (at one time, the company had British

ownership). On completion, the building was praised for its luxurious facilities, including rapid elevators, separate rooms for laundry, ironing and drying, bathrooms equipped with built-in tubs and cabinets, an in-house telephone network, and a fireproof safe in each apartment. It was also the first apartment block in Pest with eight storeys.

Saving Csontváry's paintings

Gerlóczy was looking for a good location for a studio when he chanced upon one of these buildings, which happened to be occupied by relatives of Tivadar Csontváry-Kosztka. The relatives were about to sell the canvases to be used as awning (to protect transported goods from rain), so Gerlóczy had to act quickly. Within a few days, he sold some shares that he had inherited and purchased the paintings, along with many related documents. The paintings survived the Second World War, spending decades in Gerlóczy's apartment. In the 1970s they were finally given to various museums and galleries.

PLAQUE OF THE RESTORATION OF 26,000 ROOFS

Commemorating a challenging task after the Second World War

1052 Budapest, 12-16 Városház utca
Metro: M3 – Ferenciek tere; Bus: 5, 7, 8E, 108E, 110, 112, 133E, 178 – Ferenciek tere

The siege of Budapest in 1944–45 was devastating. Following the end of the fighting, the first task was to bury all dead people and animals.

Right after this, buildings and infrastructure were to be rebuilt, especially in the inner parts of the city: In the 1st district, only four or five buildings remained intact out of 782 ...

By 1948, 26,000 roofs were restored in Budapest. A small memorial tablet reminds us of this work on the wall of the City Hall, in Városház utca.

The tablet was created by the famous ceramic artist Margit Kovács, whose works can be seen in a museum in Szentendre. The text of the tablet says: 'In 1948, the spring of the Centenary Year, under the direction and support of the Minister of Construction and Public Works, the citizens of the capital city completed the restoration of the roofs of 26,000 dwelling houses damaged in the war.'

Under the text, a map of Budapest can be seen, with its territory indicated by roof tiles. What is interesting on this map is that it shows the boundaries of a city smaller than today's: The city was extended two years later by merging several adjoining towns.

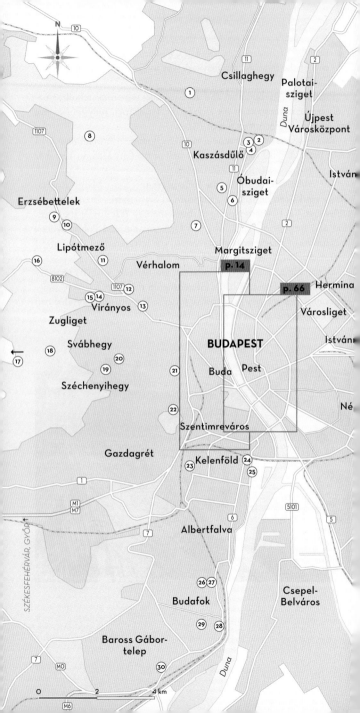

Buda

KOPPÁNY TOWER

The last remaining memory of a Neo-Pagan movement

1031 Budapest, Pogánytorony utca
Bus: 218 – Aranyvölgy vasútállomás; MÁV – Aranyvölgy

At very edge of Budapest, the half-ruined Koppány tower stands as a memento of a quite extraordinary 20th-century movement. The street name (Pogánytorony utca means Pagan tower street) refers to this building, erected by a society that wanted to see the domination of ancient Hungarian beliefs instead of Christianity. Established by Alajos Paikert in 1910, the Turanist Society (*Turáni Társaság*) was formed for the purpose of establishing cultural and economic ties with the Balkans and Asia. Paikert later became Minister of Agriculture – his supporters included Ármin Vámbéry, Lajos Lóczy and Ferenc Hopp. When Hungary formed closer ties with Turkey and Bulgaria during the First World War, the organisation gained strength, but it moved from historical research to a new kind of ideology. In place of Christianity, they wanted Hungarians to revert to ancient beliefs.

The Turanist Society claimed that every race had its own appropriate religion, and for Hungary it was Paganism. It also believed that the Turanian people of the East already had a monotheistic religion a thousand years before Moses. Pagan tribe leader Koppány was chosen as the society's guiding lord, and in support, Farkas Szász erected a tower in Aranyhegy to host pagan rites, provoking much anger in Christian churches across Hungary.

The tower was designed by architect Géza Tauber in 1933 and built the following year. When it was 'consecrated' on 7 July 1935, it drew a violent response from the police. In 1939, five white birches from the town of Törökkoppány were planted around the tower. Meetings and rituals took place here until the movement came to an end in 1942 – members of the society were deemed anticlerical and unreliable, and were sent to labour camps. In the late 1940s, the tower was taken over by the much-feared ÁVH (State Protection Authority) of the communist state.

The original plan was to erect 12 towers in Buda, but only this one ever appeared. Hexagonal in layout and about 13 metres high, it has a somewhat Romanesque style, constructed from large pieces of stone and with narrow windows. In 1935 the top of the tower was covered with a large stone slab and a statue of a Turul (a mythological bird of prey) – these have since gone missing.

When visiting, please do not climb the steps – some are missing and the top of the tower is unstable.

ÓBUDA GAS WORKS

An extraordinary abandoned factory

1031 Budapest, Gázgyár utca
Guided tours only (see Introduction for operators)
HÉV: H5 – Aquincum or Kaszásdűlő; Bus: 34, 134, 106 – Záhony utca

Closed in 1984, Óbuda Gas Works is now one of the very few major abandoned industrial sites which can officially be visited in Europe, along with Kelenföld Power Station (see p. 200). The 'chark' (charcoal or coal) incinerators and large gas containers have already been demolished. What remains today are the clock tower and the three imposing tar towers.

The first gas works in Budapest opened on 23 December 1856 in Józsefváros, supplying gas for lighting in the city centre. Four years later, a second works opened in today's Margit körút (Margit Boulevard), followed by a third in Újpest and a fourth in Ferencváros. These were purchased by the city in 1909–1910. The director of the newly formed company, Ferenc Haltai, was the first to suggest that a new larger works be built and in 1909 Óbuda was selected as the location by the Council of Budapest. The site combined proximity to cheap transportation on the Danube and to the inner city.

Prior to construction, low-lying areas were filled and a dam was built to prevent flooding. Production finally started in 1913. The works were the most modern producer of coal-based 'city gas', long before natural gas took over. Around 1,700 workers built a 'chark' incinerator with 78 chambers, 12 generators and two 57.5 metre-high gas containers, each with a capacity of a hundred thousand cubic metres. The size of the new factory meant that all four earlier factories could be closed down.

The outbreak of the First World War severely affected production. Growth was further hindered by the economic crisis of the early 1930s. In response, the Óbuda gas works expanded its product range, adding tar, pitch and naphthalene. Towards the end of the Second World War, bombing severely damaged the pipe network. When Soviet troops reached the area, they used the enormous generator, still standing in one of the buildings, to restart the supply of electricity. In the early 1950s Budapest's gas supply company (Fővárosi Gázművek) was formed. At the same time, natural gas gradually began to supersede city gas. The Óbuda works continued their inevitable decline through the 1970s and finally closed on 15 October 1984.

Following the closure of the gas works, there were several suggestions for the site's use: Some planned to open a museum, others a university. It was also part of Budapest's plans for the European Capital of Culture. After several decades of slow decay, the clock tower buildings were renovated in 2013. As the empty interiors indicate, the aim was to preserve a heritage building rather than find a new function for it.

The surrounding buildings have suffered a worse fate. New investment has been blocked by the prohibitive cost of recultivating the area's highly polluted soil. In addition, archaeological research indicates that Roman remains lie under the ground, further restricting development.

ESTATES OF THE ÓBUDA GAS FACTORY

Estates built for workers and managers

1031 Budapest, Gázgyári ltp.
Bus: 106 – Záhony utca; HÉV: H5 – Aquincum; MÁV – Aquincum

Thinking of housing estates, one normally imagines boring rows of flats, but the two estates of the former Óbuda Gas Factory are quite the opposite: They provide enchanted living environments on the outskirts of the Buda side. The estate west of the factory site was built for the workers; the one south of the factory site, along the Danube, was for the managers. In the early 20th century, large companies were regulated not only in terms of working hours and industrial standards, but they were also obliged to build homes for their workers.

The estate for the workers was designed by the architect Lóránt Almásy Balogh, a lesser-known figure of Art Nouveau. Homes on this estate, built from very simple materials, were placed around a central green zone planted with plane trees, which made for a strong sense of community among

the workers. Each home, even on the upper levels, had access to a small garden, and the estate even had an integrated kindergarten. Workers were also provided with local amenities: a hairdresser, bakery, cinema, pharmacy, etc., along with a bus service to help with the shopping. The kindergarten survived, but the opening of a nearby hypermarket ruined the other businesses. During the First World War, workers were allowed to keep animals in the gardens. Occasionally, in happier times, the director would join the workers in dancing at a ball.

South of the factory site is where the villas of the factory managers were built right by a beautiful tree-lined promenade in Almási Balogh Lóránd utca, designed by Kálmán Reichl, one of the architects of the Kelenföld power station (see p. 200). The largest apartment – number VII, 450 square metres – belonged to the director. Some of the smaller villas incorporated two apartments, each with access to a spacious garden. The buildings here are much more elaborate than those for the workers.

Some of the older current tenants used to work in the factory, and the director's chauffeur became a tenant of villa VII. Both estates are protected heritage sites.

ANCIENT ROMAN DOG PAWS ④

Probably the coolest reception desk in Budapest

Offices of Graphisoft Park
1031 Budapest, Záhony utca
Open during working hours
Bus: 106 – Záhony utca; HÉV: H5 – Kaszásdűlő

Behind the ancient ruins of Aquincum (one of the most visited tourist attractions in Budapest) are the modern offices of Graphisoft Park. In 2017 a new reception building ('I') was opened, featuring a truly unique reception desk which serves as a display case for 140 ancient Roman bricks that were found in the office park during its construction.

When taking a closer look, animal footprints can be seen on several bricks. They were left in the clay almost two thousand years ago by Roman dogs when a pottery operated here: The clay bricks were probably left out in the sun to dry and the dogs happily trotted across them, leaving their marks for millennia – and putting a smile on the faces of today's office workers.

HERCULES VILLA ⑤

Magnificent mosaics from Roman times

1033 Budapest, 21 Meggyfa utca
aquincum.hu/en/a-muzeumrol/budapest-romai-emlekei/hercules-villa
1 April - 31 Oct, Tue–Sun 10am–6pm
Bus: 9, 34, 109, 111, 118, 134 – Óbuda, Bogdáni út

Behind the large housing blocks of Óbuda, the remains of the Hercules Villa, dating from the first half of the second century CE, contain beautiful Roman mosaics and the remaining ancient walls of the villa. It's just a short walk from the Bogdáni út terminus of several bus lines. These vestiges were unearthed in the middle of the last century, while digging the foundations for a new school building in Meggyfa utca. To protect the remains, two small buildings were erected.

Beneath the longest roof, the most valuable mosaic depicts a scene from the myth of Hercules and Deianira, the only known mosaic artwork imported from outside the province of Pannonia, probably created in a workshop in Alexandria. The complete image comprised approximately 60,000 pieces.

Also on show within the cellar level of the school building are the remains of a *tablinum* (family room), where the mosaic is bordered by geometric patterns. Half of the middle section is a reconstruction based on existing patterns. The other half has collapsed into the structure of the floor heating. The complete image was of a procession held in honour of Dionysus (also known as Bacchus), the god of wine, depicting a drinking competition between Hercules and Dionysus, with Hercules being the loser. A tiger, the animal attributed to Dionysus, also appears in the mosaic, together with Cupid offering a bunch of grapes.

A smaller building, made up of triangular concrete panels and glass walls, protects the bathing area. Mosaic tiles found in the *apodyterium* (changing room) depict a boxing match. The winner stands triumphant, while his opponent is knocked out and bleeding from the head. Gravestones in the yard indicate that the building was abandoned sometime around the 3rd or 4th century CE, and that the site was used as a burial ground.

FORMER SILK MANUFACTURE IN ÓBUDA

⑥

A beautiful and rare oval building

1033 Budapest, 1 Miklós tér
madgardenbuda.hu
Bus: 9, 109, 118, 218 - Raktár utca

One of the lesser-known old buildings of Budapest, the historic building of the silk manufacture in Óbuda has an out of the ordinary shape: a rectangle with two semi-circles on its shorter sides. Surrounded by old trees and concealing a small inner yard on two levels, the baroque-era building has a unique atmosphere.

Entrance is from the two oval ends of the building, through a small front yard.

In the original setup there were no dividing walls so that the work could be easily surveyed from the courtyard: There were 28 work stations along the outer perimeter and 16 inside. The unique-shaped layout made it possible to have a good overview on all the work stations at the same time.

The building itself dates from the 18th century when Joseph II, Holy Roman Emperor from 1765 until his death in 1790, decided to promote the development of industry in the Habsburg monarchy, including the production of silk fibre. In 1781 he invited Italian professional Agostino Mazzocato to assist in setting up a factory in Hungary, following plans from architect József Tallherr. The factory began operating in 1786, also functioning as a training centre for workers. Following Mazzocato's death in 1814, his son inherited the business. Later, silk factory owner Károly Roscogni became director until production ended in 1830. The building survived the flood in 1838 (see p. 106), but was almost completely abandoned. It was sold by the Treasury, and the new owner converted it into apartments with a gallery on the upper level. After the Second World War, the building was restored in the 1950s, then again in the 1980s, when it was converted into a cultural centre.

Today, the space is occupied by offices and the courtyard by a beer garden from spring to autumn.

© fortepan.hu, Stipkovits Fülöp

THE 'ORTHODOX' PAINTINGS OF KISCELLI MUSEUM

Are they as ancient as they look?

1037 Budapest, 108 Kiscelli utca
kiscellimuzeum.hu
Tue –Sun 10am–6pm, closed Mondays: Nov–Mar Tue–Fri only 10am–4pm
Tram: 17, 19, 41 – Szent Margit kórház

Housed in an old castle on a steep Óbuda hillside, the Kiscelli Museum features hidden spaces that even regular visitors frequently miss, like the area beneath the former chapel of the castle that currently functions as an exhibition area. Below the chapel, the far less well-known cellar level is one of those hidden areas. Some of its walls and columns are decorated with images that seem to be ancient Orthodox paintings. But the castle is not that old, and the images are indeed not that old either…

The paintings date from 1994, when an event organised by the Anastasia Foundation (created to promote the rebirth of traditional religious practices), titled 'Pas d'accord avec Zeffirelli' (not OK with Zeffirelli), brought together five Romanian artists: Sorin Dumitrescu, Mihai Sârbulescu, Horea Paştina, Ion Grigorescu and Ioana Bătrânu. Using ancient techniques to paint icons on the walls, the artists created the Orthodox-themed works. At the same time, scenes from Franco Zeffirelli's 1977 TV mini-series Jesus of Nazareth played on screens in the background. The aim of the event was to contrast Christian traditions with the modern international interpretation of Christianity.

The crypt can be seen in a fight scene in the 2019 movie Gemini Man, starring Will Smith.

The former chapel of the castle

In the 1720s, a chapel was built in Óbuda by count Péter Zichy to house a copy of the Virgin Mary statue in Mariazell. In 1738 monks of the Trinitarian order arrived and between 1744 and 1749 a monastery was built for them. The order was dissolved in 1784, the furnishings were auctioned off and the monastery church was converted into military barracks. In 1910, Viennese furniture manufacturer and art collector Max Schmidt (also known as Miksa Schmidt) purchased the site and used the church to display his art collection. According to his will, the castle was to be inherited by the capital city. Thereafter, the city tried to display the collection of the Municipal Museum here, but the building suffered severe damage in the Second World War, so the first exhibition did not open until 1948. The church was converted into an exhibition area as recently as 1989.

THE OLD CHURCH OF GERCSE

A true little gem on the edge of the city

1028 Budapest, Gercsényi utca
pesthidegkutiplebania.hu
Open before Sunday Mass at 5pm
Bus: 64, 164, 264 – Mikszáth Kálmán utca; or Volánbusz from Hűvösvölgy

The small village of Gercse is today part of the 2nd district and home to one of the oldest churches in Budapest, unknown even to most locals. The calm and historical atmosphere of the place makes it a true little gem on the edge of the city.

Built at the end of the 13th century, the church has one nave, no tower, and a horseshoe-shaped shrine. It was destroyed at least twice in the Middle Ages and again in 1595 during the Turkish occupation. In 1774 German settlers from the Rhine area rebuilt it and included Baroque elements; the nave was extended west, and a balcony was added for the organ, along with a vestry. It was still standing in 1817, but records from 1827 describe it in ruins.

Archaeological research in 1985 revealed that the church was once enclosed by a wall 60 x 60 metres long and 70 centimetres thick. The remains of this wall can still be found below ground level. An extensive rebuild in 1996–1997, including new benches and a new altar, has restored the atmosphere of the early Middle Ages to this modest place of worship.

THE TRAIN SHED
OF THE CHILDREN'S RAILWAY

A Skoda converted into a railcar

Hűvösvölgy station
1029 Budapest, Hűvösvölgy
gyermekvasut.hu
Open during special events only, see website
Tram: 56, 56A, 59B, 61 – Hűvösvölgy

If the Children's Railway line is a popular tourist attraction, a much less well-known shed at Hűvösvölgy station houses some items related to the line from the communist period. As it is still fully operational, it is only open during special events (see above).

The main attractions are the old locomotives and passenger carriages, many of which came from other narrow-gauge railways in the countryside: The Mk-49 locomotives, for instance, are from the town of Sárospatak. But the most unique vehicle is probably a Skoda, produced in 1948 and converted into a railcar in 1949. After serving in Sárospatak and Hanság, this unusual vehicle was stored in Sopron and in Celldömölk before arriving here in 2003. It now has the engine of a Lada and a new number: Pft-272.

The old station signs also ended up in the shed, where they are occasionally displayed. They remind us of the old communist era station names (see opposite).

The world's longest children's railway

Opened in 1948–1950, the Gyermekvasút (Children's Railway) or Line 7 is a narrow gauge railway line in Budapest that connects Széchenyihegy and Hűvösvölgy and is 11.7 kilometres long.

The former name of the line was *Úttörővasút* (Pioneer Railway, in reference to the communist scouts).

Except for the train driver, all of the posts are filled by children aged 10–14, operating under adult supervision, like the original concept imagined in Soviet times. It is the world's longest children's railway.

Several station names along the line referred to the ideology of the times: Úttörőváros (Pioneer Town) – close to the large pioneer camp of Csillebérc, today named Csillebérc; Előre (Forward), today named Virágvölgy, meaning Flower Valley; and Ságvári Liget (Ságvári Grove), named after Endre Ságvári, a communist activist of the time, today named Szépjuhászné.

These stations were renamed in 1990 at the same time that the railway became known the Children's Railway.

Between the train shed and the terminal, there is a small turntable: Locomotives are turned on it from time to time to make sure that the abrasion on the wheels is even.

THE UNFINISHED HUNGARIAN HOLY LAND CHURCH

Bringing the wonders of the Holy Land to Hungary

1021 Budapest, 3 Heinrich István utca
Guided tours only (see Introduction for operators)
Tram: 56, 56A, 59B, 61 – Heinrich István utca

Behind a large gate at the end of a path leading off Heinrich István utca stands an elliptical building with a concrete colonnade. It is one of the last works by Farkas Molnár, a Hungarian member of the Bauhaus. This unique unfinished and abandoned building can be visited with a guided tour only (see above).

In 1937 Molnár got to know János Mór Majsai, a Franciscan monk and head of the Hungarian Holy Land Commission. During the 1930s, both Majsai and Molnár visited Palestine to research sacred sites as Molnár planned to build replicas of the holy sites in Hungary.

In 1940 the foundations of the building were laid, and construction began in 1942 following approval by the Catholic Church. The main block was to be split into smaller chapels, each with curved walls at the front and back. A copy of the Holy Grave (the tomb where Jesus' body was laid after his crucifixion) was to be placed in the inner yard. By the end of 1944, some of the chapels were complete. A few months later, Molnár died and oversight of the construction passed to Jenő Szendrői.

Following the communist takeover in 1949, construction came to a halt. The dome, already partly built, was dismantled and the chapels were vandalised. In later decades, the spaces were used for warehousing, or as artists' studios. Budapest City Archives eventually acquired the building for storage purposes, but moved out in 2004. Since then, the building has stood abandoned. The empty, unfinished church has been owned by the Franciscans since 2013.

All that remains is the elliptical main block, 40 metres long by 25 metres wide, with outer walls and inner columns. Around the walls are two rows of window cavities. The main entrance, intended to be a replica of the Church of the Holy Sepulchre, is today just another unrealised part of the project.

Entry is limited to occasional guided tours, but much of the building can be viewed from the outside.

On the neighbouring plot (accessed from Hűvösvölgyi út), a replica 'Lourdes Chapel' can be seen, also in a rather dilapidated condition.

NAPRAFORGÓ UTCA ESTATE

A beautiful little street full of early modern villas

1021 Budapest, Napraforgó utca
napraforgoutca.hu
Occasional guided tours (see Introduction for operators)
Tram: 56, 56A, 59B, 61 – Zuhatag sor

Running parallel to the tramline on the way to Hűvösvölgy, Napraforgó utca is a small street that offers an insight into how we once thought the future might look. In the late 1920s there was intense discourse about a new kind of architecture and modernity: Napraforgó utca (Sunflower Street) is the result of an experiment to put theory into practice.

All nineteen units (sixteen houses and three dual-apartment buildings) were built in under twelve months in 1931, drawing heavily on the desire for healthy, practical, affordable and sustainable housing. The Association of Hungarian Engineers and Architects already had a reference point for the project: the Weissenhof Estate in Stuttgart, Germany.

As several architects were involved, some differences in style can be found: Some houses follow the principles of the Bauhaus movement; others those of Art Deco; and one features elements of Neo-Baroque. Yet there is harmony: Most of the buildings' outer walls are painted a single colour, have flat roofs and (with few exceptions) two floors. The colours are strong and bright, much bolder than commonly used today. Recently, the majority of the fences have been rebuilt following the original plans, with lighting integrated into the supporting columns. Past reconstructions have resulted in the loss of several original elements, or incongruous sheds and such. However, the current owners strive to maintain the buildings' original appeal.

A small square in the middle of the street contains a monument that lists the names of the architects of each house. Included are such 'star' architects of the times as Lajos Kozma, József Fischer, Alfréd Hajós and Farkas Molnár.

IMRE NAGY MEMORIAL HOUSE

Memories of the prime minister of 1956

1026 Budapest, 43 Orsó utca
392 5011, 392 5012
Mon–Fri 10am–4pm
Free entry – booking for guided tours: tarlatvezetes@nagyimrealapitvany.hu
For regular conferences and other events see nagyimreemlekhaz.hu
Bus: 5 – Pasaréti tér

Although Imre Nagy is a well-known figure of the 1956 revolution, the house where he lived doesn't receive many visitors, probably because of its relatively remote location, outside the city centre. The house is now dedicated to the preservation of his memory as a leading figure of the 1956 revolution that broke out against Soviet rule in Hungary.

Designed by renowned architect Lajos Kozma, just a few blocks from Pasaréti tér, the villa was built in 1931–32. It was here that the chairman of the Council of Ministers (de facto prime minister) wrote his parliamentary speech that laid down the foundations of the 1953 government programme. He also wrote his thesis here, published later in the book titled *In defence of the Hungarian people*. This is also the family home that he left in the evening of 23 October 1956 – the day the revolution broke out.

On 4 November, he tried to save his family's life by finding refuge in the embassy of Yugoslavia, only to be finally captured, subjected to a show trial and executed on 16 June 1958. His body (together with others executed at that time) was exhumed in 1989. Their re-burial became an emblematic event of the fall of communism in Hungary.

In 1990, a foundation was created to maintain the memory of the former country leader, and the Memorial House opened in 2002. Since the possessions of the Nagy family were confiscated by the State at that time, and because the villa has had several new tenants after 1956, the exhibition could initially display only a few original objects. In 2008 a new modern exhibition was created, with hundreds of photos and dozens of videos.

The memory of the missing objects (details of the old bookshelf, a chair, a philodendron, the end of a bed) has been evoked by carving them out of white plaster. An exception to this is the reconstruction of the former offices, where the prime minister once worked.

STATUE OF RAOUL WALLENBERG ⑬

*A statue commemorating a disappeared diplomat
who saved thousands of Jews*

1026 Budapest, 101 Szilágyi Erzsébet fasor
*Tram: 56, 56A, 59, 59B, 61 – Nagyajtai utca; Bus: 91, 291 – Gábor Áron utca
or Szilágyi Erzsébet fasor*

On a patch of green land at the junction of Szilágyi Erzsébet fasor and Nagyajtai utca stands a statue showing a figure of a man amongst two large upright granite slabs. The two slabs are not mere background; they work specifically to obscure the figure when passing by. Imre Varga (1923–2019) designed the piece to represent the disappearance of Swedish diplomat and humanitarian Raoul Wallenberg in January 1945. The granite was a gift from the Wallenberg family and was selected by Varga himself in Sweden.

Raoul Wallenberg, of the famous Wallenberg family, was a Swedish diplomat who worked in Budapest during the Second World War. He saved thousands of Jewish lives by issuing 'protective passports' that provided them with the protection of a foreign country. At the end of the war, when the Red Army captured Budapest, the Soviets took Wallenberg prisoner. His car was found close to where the statue stands today. Throughout the following decades, Moscow remained silent; there was no explanation for the diplomat's arrest. In 1947 the Soviet Foreign Minister announced that Wallenberg was not in the Soviet Union. Ten years later, another announcement confirmed that he had died in a Moscow prison in July 1947.

The first Wallenberg memorial was created by Pál Pátzay. It depicts a man overpowering a snake. Pátzay was Varga's teacher and friend, and as an act of remembrance, Varga carved an image of Pátzay's statue across the granite slabs. It is encompassed by a quote from Ovid: 'Donec eris felix, multos numerabis amicos / Tempora si fuerint nubila, solus eris' – meaning 'As long as you are fortunate, you will have many friends / If cloudy times appear, you will be alone.'

Varga was rather brave to depict Wallenberg as an old man, wearing the typical clothes of Soviet labour camps: drugget cloak and clogs. The statue was first erected in 1985 in the garden of the United States Embassy in Budapest – i.e. on American territory. It was the diplomatic pressure put on Hungarian communist leader Kádár by the Swedish and the American ambassadors that finally led to the erection of the statue in its current location. The 1987 inauguration was as low key as possible, with no announcements in newspapers, just one week before Kádár's visit to Sweden.

# TWO SECTIONS
OF THE BERLIN WALL

⑭

A reminder of a forgotten moment when East Germans crossed the border before the fall of the Berlin Wall

Garden of the Hungarian Charity Service of the Order of Malta in Zugliget
1125 Budapest, 58-60 Szarvas Gábor út
Bus: 291 – Szarvas Gábor út

In communist times, there were strict limits as to where East Germans could travel – socialist Hungary was one of the few permitted places. Budapest and Lake Balaton were popular destinations, but the summer of 1989 proved to be very different. In February of that year, as a sign of improving relations, Hungary and Austria reached an agreement to remove the 'iron curtain' of barbed wire, landmines and the electric signalling systems designed to prevent border crossings. By June, the last section of the fence had been removed. The Berlin Wall, however, remained strong.

Taking advantage of this situation, tens of thousands of East Germans came to Hungary, leading to the largest refugee crisis of the time in Europe. On 14 August 1989, the Order of Malta Charity Service opened the first refugee shelter for many of these people, and over the next three months, across several sites (further camps were opened in Hárshegy and Csillebérc), more than 48,600 people arrived in Budapest. Led by Father Imre Kozma, co-founder of the Hungarian Charity Service of the Order of Malta, the programme was supported by West Germany.

Most of the refugees were unwilling to leave the camps, as members of the *Stasi* (East German secret police) were seen photographing them from neighbouring rooftops. On 19 August, during an event called the Pan-European Picnic, the borders were opened up for a few hours, enabling hundreds of East Germans to cross the border. The Hungarian-Austrian border was finally fully opened up for East Germans on 14 November, and the remaining refugees made their way across.

On 9 November 1989, the Berlin Wall finally came down. Two sections of the wall were donated to the SZDSZ, a liberal party in Hungary. The sections were initially installed in Tabán Park, but when people began removing pieces of them (someone even repainted them dark red), a decision was made to move them to a safer place. Since 2004, the sections have stood in the garden of the Maltese Charity Service in Zugliget. Many people still visit from Germany, including former refugees and diplomats.

Father Kozma could not relax for very long: In December of 1989, the revolution broke out in Romania, putting an end to Nicolai Ceausescu's dictatorship. The Order of Malta Charity Service took part in the collection and distribution of donations.

THE TRAM TERMINUS
IN ZUGLIGET

The former terminus of a horse-drawn tram line

1121 Budapest, 64 Zugligeti út
helytortenetigyujtemeny.hu
lovasut.hu
Wed–Sun 10am–6pm
Bus: 291 – Zugligeti út

Far from the city centre, but close to hiking trails and the 'Libegő' chairlift, the building at 64 Zugligeti út was once the terminus of a horse-drawn tram line. It features elaborate wooden decorations, brick walls and – since its latest renovation a few years ago – an exhibition space for the local historical collection of the 12th district.

Zugliget became a popular tourist destination in the 1830s, and in 1832 one of the first omnibus services in Buda began taking passengers here from the centre. This was later replaced by a horse-drawn tram line in 1868, which was itself replaced by electric trams in 1896. The tramline was finally closed down in 1977 and replaced by a bus service. The tram terminal building was designed by József Kauser, inspired by alpine architecture and the nearby early 19th-century holiday homes. Built in 1868, the brick structure consisted of two pavilions connected by a central courtyard, all under a long roof. In the 1920s, the courtyard was walled up and developed to provide homes for workers. Following its renovation in 2017 by Zoboki Design and Architecture (well known in Hungary for the design of MüPa), a glass wall now indicates the once open area. Behind the building is a new extension. All the viable pieces were used in the restoration, while any missing parts were reproduced from original drawings, paying attention to even the smallest details of the intricate wood, cast-iron and brick decorations.

On 4 June 1900, passengers in the electric tram accidentally removed the brakes of their carriage: It accelerated quickly on the steep hillside and derailed on a bend at Virányosi út. Four of the seventy passengers died and nine were hospitalised with serious injuries. As a consequence of the accident, ticket inspectors were obliged to regularly check the brakes and a new terminal station was built on a flat area farther up the hill, where Niche Camping is today.

THE MOSAIC
OF SZÉPJUHÁSZNÉ STATION

A forgotten vestige from the Soviet era

In the proximity of 1021 Budapest, 93 Budakeszi út
Bus: 22, 22A, 222, Children's Railway – Szépjuhászné

Few people who visit the famous Children's Railway (see p. 166) venture around the railway itself, which explains why very few people know of the beautiful mosaic that adorns Szépjuhászné station on the Children's Railway. Created by Ferenc Jánossy, it depicts an idealised image from the Soviet era: a happy family walking among the trees of a forest, the father holding a large red flag in his hand. Two birds symbolise peace. At the bottom of the mosaic, a symbolic image of the railway can be seen.

Built in the Stalinist era of communism in Hungary, following the creation of similar railway lines in the Soviet Union, the railway line itself was called the Pioneers' Railway. Several stations were decorated in the compulsory, state-enforced style of socialist realism, but only a few of these artworks remain today. The example at Szépjuhászné station is among the most beautiful.

NEARBY

The ruins of Budaszentlőrinc monastery
Open all year

Near the Children's Railway, hidden behind large trees, the ruins of Saint Paul's monastery are largely forgotten. What we can see today, however, is a reconstruction of the original layout, based on 20th-century archaeological research.

The monastery was built in the 14th century by the Order of Saint Paul, the only Catholic order that was established in Hungary, in honour of Saint Paul the Hermit (i.e. Paul of Thebes) who lived in the 3rd century CE. After receiving the Pope's approval in 1308, the construction of the monastery began with financial support from the King of Hungary. It was dedicated to St Lawrence (Szent Lőrinc), hence the name of the old village: Budaszentlőrinc.

The church of the monastery had three naves and was 49 metres long and 14 metres wide. In 1526, most of the 300–500 monks left Budaszentlőrinc, fleeing the Turkish army. The remaining few dozen monks were killed, and the monastery was partly destroyed. When Buda was taken back from the Turks in 1686, the stones of the monastery were used during the city's reconstruction. This meant the final destruction of the monastery.

MAKOVECZ CENTRE AND ARCHIVES

A beautiful little-known example of organic architecture

1125 Budapest, 2 Városkúti út
+36 (70) 330 1719
makovecz.hu
Mon, Wed and Fri 2pm–5pm
Free – booking for group visits: office@makovecz.hu
Bus: 128 – Regőczi István tér

Designed to be the architect's own family house (unfortunately Imre Makovecz died before he could move in), the Makovecz Centre and Archives is a signature building by the master of Hungarian organic architecture.

With its extraordinary interiors, strange curves and high quality wooden structures, the centre is the perfect place to learn about his oeuvre. Somewhat secluded from the street, and in a curious horseshoe layout structure, the building boasts a transparent veranda that encircles a walnut tree at its centre, allowing sunlight to shine through during the day. The architect's plan was to plant fruit trees in the back yard. In a neighbouring room, the architect's study was installed: His furniture, books and personal objects were brought here from his former office at 25 Kecske utca.

Used by the Imre Makovecz Foundation, the building also hosts meetings, presentations and lectures.

Imre Makovecz: a master of organic architecture in Budapest

Organic architecture is a philosophy of architecture which promotes harmony between human habitation and the natural world. Coined by architect Frank Lloyd Wright (1867–1959), its main representatives have since been Louis Sullivan and Rudolf Steiner. Imre Makovecz (1935–2011) was the leading figure of organic architecture in Hungary. His architecture was backed by a strong theoretical way of thinking, rejecting communism and globalism and seeking inspiration in the folk culture of Hungary. He had many followers, founded an association (the Károly Kós Association), organised an architecture school for young professionals and started the Country Builder (*Országépítő*) magazine.

He became famous with his early works built in the Visegrád hills for the forestry. On an international level, his greatest success was probably the pavilion of the Seville Expo, held in 1992 (see *Secret Seville*, from the same publisher). His works can be found all over the Carpathian basin, stretching beyond the boundaries of Hungary, and ranging from schools to churches to cultural centres.

Works of Imre Makovecz in Budapest

The lookout tower on Hárshegy (1021 Budapest, Hárshegyi körút), was built in wood in 1982. It is a small but unique structure, forming a double spiral.

The mortuary located close to the main entrance of the Farkasrét Cemetery (1124 Budapest, 99 Németvölgyi út) was completed in 1977. He designed the interiors using curved pieces of wood, creating the impression of the ribs of the chest of a man. The dead body in the coffin is placed where the heart is found inside the chest. The gates of the hall are shaped like angel wings – this is the first appearance of the motif, repeated many times in the architect's later works. After his death, his final farewells were made here in 2011.

The Church of Togetherness, a Protestant church in Pesterzsébet-Szabótelep (1202 Budapest, 149 Mártírok útja), was designed by Makovecz but his death in 2011 stopped construction. One of his apprentices, Tamás Dósa Papp, then finished it in 2021. The building became larger than originally planned, with an additional hall that can house events. The church looks like it is growing out of the soil, while the roof seems to descend from the skies – fulfilling Makovecz's vision of churches connecting Earth and Heaven.

The Ascension Church in Rákoskert (1171 Budapest, 22 Tiszaörs utca), Makovecz laid the foundation stone of in 2009, but the church was only completed after his death.

In 2005, Makovecz planned the large St Michael and the Resurrection Church, to be built in Apor Vilmos tér. Lacking financial support and dedication from the Catholic Church, this plan – often described as the peak of his oeuvre – remained unrealised.

THE SVÁBHEGY OBSERVATORY

Where the sky is not the limit

Planet Earth, 1121 Budapest, 15-17 Konkoly-Thege Miklós út
svabhegyicsillagvizsgalo.hu – info@svabhegyicsillagvizsgalo.hu
Guided tours are available for groups, with prior booking, during the day or
after sunset
Bus: 21 – Csillagvizsgáló

In the proximity of Normafa, one of the greenest areas in Budapest, at the very end of the city, the Svábhegy observatory boasts a neo-classicist style building (1926) right by the entrance. It is home to the offices of the researchers, but above all, invisible from the street, there are three

observatory buildings that can be found in the greenery of the backyard. With prior booking, they are open to the public.

The largest dome hosts a telescope built in 1928 by the German company Heyde: the largest telescope in the country at that time. The hemispheric dome features a beautiful wooden-clad interior, a copper-clad roof and an openable section. The entire dome is placed on glide rails. It is named 'Budapest dome', because the municipality of Budapest financed a significant part of its construction. The telescope is placed on a base that is separated from the building itself so that no vibration hinders the observations.

Built in 1922, the Meridian House includes the instruments that once measured the position of the sun. Until the 1930s, the exact time was transmitted from here to the Hungarian State Railways. In the auditorium, named after Kunó Klebelsberg, former minister of culture, a meteorite analysis lab was installed. Visitors can touch actual pieces of rock from outer space, and wonder at their colourful crystal structures under a microscope.

A road to the stars

The road of the observatory is named after Miklós Konkoly-Thege, a rich nobleman who built his first observatory on his estate in Ógyalla in 1869. In 1899, he handed over the observatory to the Hungarian state and became the first director of the *Astrophysikai Observatorium* until his death in 1916.

With the signing of the Trianon peace treaty in 1920, Hungary lost about two thirds of its territory: Ógyalla became a part of the newly formed Czechoslovakia and is today part of Slovakia (the observatory, located in Hurbanovo (Hungarian: Ógyalla) in Slovakia, is still working and is open to visitors).

In a clever move, the equipment was sent to Budapest just before, in 1919, laying the foundations for the observatory on the peak of Svábhegy.

The first observatory in Budapest was set up in the Citadel in 1815, but it was damaged during the siege of Buda in 1849, and later closed down.

SZÉCHENYI GLORIETTE

The gloriette that stood on Heroes' Square before the Millennium Monument

1121 Budapest, 12 Széchenyi-emlék út
Cog-wheel Railway (60) – Művész út

On the outskirts of Buda, on the side of Széchenyi Hill, far away from the noise of the city centre, the Széchenyi gloriette features two wide staircases leading to an upper terrace, and a large flagpole in its centre.

The gloriette hasn't always been here: It used to stand on Heroes' Square before the Millennium Monument did. After finding thermal water in Városliget park in the late 19th century, the spring needed to be protected: The city's Graphic Arts Committee commissioned Miklós Ybl in 1884 to design a temporary structure. Inside the structure, a dome covered the pipes, while on two sides curved staircases led to a hexagonal terrace.

Between the rails of the stairs, a water fountain was placed. Vases were arranged at the corners and a large circular pedestal was set in the centre. The pedestal supported a 24-metre flagpole decorated with wreaths and griffins. The structure acquired the nickname 'toothpick'.

Around the turn of the century, major construction got underway, including the Museum of Fine Arts (1906), the Millennium Monument (1906) and the Hall of Arts (1896). This meant that the gloriette had to go. But it wasn't demolished, only relocated.

It was rebuilt in 1926 on Széchenyi Hill in the 12th district, where it remains today (minus the fountain). A bust of Széchenyi stands in front of the monument.

The dolphins of the gloriette
The two sculpted dolphins positioned at the end of each staircase hark back to the former fountain of the monument.

JÓKAI GARDEN

Birds, trees, wine and contentment on a steep hillside

1121 Budapest, 21 Költő utca
dunaipoly.hu/en/places/interpretation-sites/jokai-natural-garden
Guided group visits only, phone or email to book: 30 663-4670 or kovaria@
dinpi.hu
Bus: 110, 112 – Tamási Áron utca / Thomán István utca or 21, 21A, 60 –
Svábhegy; Cog-wheel railway: 60 – Svábhegy

Jókai Garden, which can only be visited as part of a group on a guided tour, is a beautiful and little-known place that features a vineyard, a centre for ornithology, a splendid view over the city, and a memorial room to the writer Mór Jókai, a famous 19th-century Hungarian writer. Jókai was so fond of nature that he bought a large empty plot on the hillside of Svábhegy in 1853 with the proceeds of his popular novel *Egy magyar nábob* (A Hungarian *nabob*). He and his wife transformed the site, planting fruit trees and a vineyard around their new villa. It remained in the family until 1922.

In the Second World War, the villa suffered bomb damage, and after several changes of ownership, it was eventually demolished. In 1960 a new office building was erected in its place, but the cellar and garden remained. In 1968 the space was dedicated to the writer.

Once through the main gate, the path leads to a stone bench where Jókai loved to sit and write often about the garden, the plants, the changing seasons, the nesting birds, etc. He planted grapes and kept farm animals: chickens, cows, pigs and a donkey. The office building also includes a small exhibition about the birds of Hungary. Opposite the building, a small rose garden offers a wonderful panorama of the city.

Across the road, steep steps lead directly to the cellar and a small exhibition about Jókai, and behind a wooden building a little further on, the steep slope is used for vines. A small display of rocks, arranged by the national park according to their geological age, guides visitors back to the entrance.

The best time to visit the Jókai Garden is in the autumn, when the grape harvest festival is in full flow.

Jókai loved his garden so much that he even wanted to be buried here. Built like a garden, with a stone bench, his grave is actually in Kerepesi Cemetery. Under the nearby trees is a statue by sculptor József Róna of the Greek lyric poet Anacreon. The face of the happy old man is modelled on Jókai's own.

CYRILLIC INSCRIPTION AT BEETHOVEN UTCA

The house 'free of mines'

1126 Budapest, 11 Beethoven utca
Bus: 102, 212 – Királyhágó tér; Tram: 59, 59A, 59B – Királyhágó tér

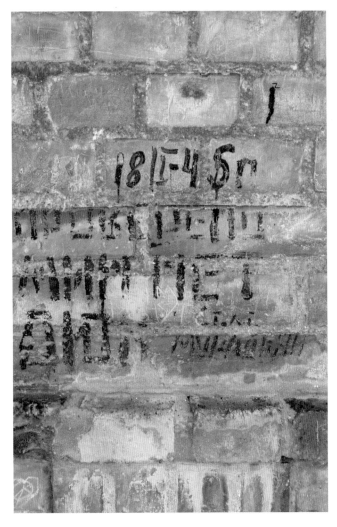

The small house at 11 Beethoven utca has an inscription painted on it in Cyrillic script. It is one of the few remaining signs left by the Red Army on many buildings at the end of the Second World War.

Towards the end of the war, houses had to be checked for unexploded bombs or mines. Once a building had been cleared, a short message was painted on the wall, declaring it free of mines (*мин нет*). The inscription also notes the military general responsible for checking – in this case, Sokholov (*Соколов*). It also states the name of the squadron responsible – here, Seno (*Сено*) probably refers to Széna tér. Since the date was included, the signs also serve as a record of the advancing front as Budapest was occupied building by building in the bloody winter of 1944–1945.

Since 1945, most of these inscriptions have disappeared as old buildings were pulled down or renovated. Here a few that still exist:
- 11 Beethoven utca
- 6 Semsey Andor utca
- 5/a Csilla utca
- 8/a Buday László utca
There may be others.

SAS HILL

A hidden nature reserve offering a great panorama

1112 Budapest, 24 Tájék utca
dunaipoly.hu/en
See website for opening hours
Bus: 8E – Korompai utca

Even if its bright rocks can be seen from many parts of the city, the Sas Hill is nonetheless a hidden nature reserve that offers breathtaking views of Budapest. Its peak, 266 metres above sea level, is a protected area.

A bus from the city centre stops at Korompai utca, from where Tájék utca leads to the entrance of the reserve. There are no large trees as the soil is too thin, but the flora and fauna include several species that live only here in Hungary and survived the last ice age. Renowned scientists such as Pál Kitaibel, Ottó Herman and János Balogh have studied the unique wildlife and geology of this special hill.

Despite awareness of the need to protect this area being highlighted in the early 20th century, it didn't become a nature reserve until 1958. In 1974–75 a fence was built around it, along with paths and a visitor centre – the current building came later.

Though the wildlife here is on the small side, it still has its wonders: spiders that exist nowhere else in the world, rare bugs and butterflies. European copper skinks and Caspian whipsnakes can also be found on the hill.

THE CHURCH OF
KÜLSŐ-KELENFÖLD PARISH

A modern church that looks like it came from a 1970s sci-fi film

1115 Budapest, 1 Ildikó tér
Sundays 9:30am – service at 10am
Metro: M4 – Kelenföld; Tram: 19, 49, 56A – Kelenföld vasútállomás; Bus: 103 – Kelenföld vasútállomás

Hidden in Ildikó square, within walking distance of the Kelenföld transport hub, is the amazing futuristic church of Külső-Kelenföld Parish. One of the few churches built during Hungary's socialist era, it looks like a spaceship straight out of a 1970s science fiction film.

Surrounded by small apartment houses on one side and multi-storey concrete buildings on the other, the church was designed by the architect István Szabó. Szabó specialised in exhibition halls and pavilions, but turned towards church architecture in his later years. He supervised the construction of the church between 1979 and 1981.

As the head architect of Hungexpo 1968, Szabó registered a patent for the construction of large grid structures, such as that used in Ildikó square. The concrete foundations measure just one metre; above them, galvanised steel pipes provide the main structure, based on a hexagonal layout angled at 45 degrees.

Despite its relatively small size, the church interior is impressive and spacious. Light pours in from one sloping side where the pipe structure is combined with a glass pane. The hexagonal 'roof' originally had glass windows, which were later replaced with polycarbonate sheets during renovations. The three branches of the belfry symbolise the Holy Trinity, while its electromagnetic equipment functions as a chime.

Szabó designed two other churches in Budapest: one in Farkasrét, opposite the main entrance of the cemetery, and another at the Forgách utca metro station on the M3 line.

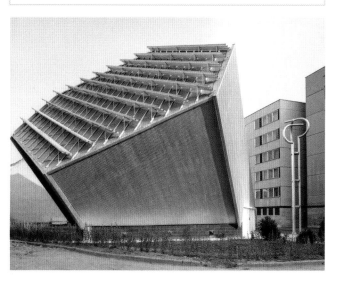

TECHNICAL STUDY STORES

A treasure trove for vintage technology enthusiasts

Hungarian Museum of Science, Technology and Transport
1117 Budapest, 10 Prielle Kornélia utca
facebook.com/MuszakiTanulmanytar – tunde.jolathy@kozlekedesimuzeum.hu
Only group visits available, bookings by email
Bus: 33, 133E – Budafoki út/Dombóvári út; Tram: 1, 41 – Hauszmann Alajos
utca/Szerémi út

Opened in 2006, the Technical Study Stores of the Hungarian Museum of Science, Technology and Transport incorporate three large halls containing storage racks packed with around 16,000 items, many of which are on display. The breathtakingly varied collection is a treasure trove for vintage technology enthusiasts.

Old telescopes from the Konkoly-Thege Observatory are on display in the first hall, with a television camera from the 1950s, a set of glass eyes, optics and film and TV recording equipment.

In the second hall are two ancient computers. On one side, placed on a desk, is the MESZ-1, the very first Hungarian computer. Assembled at the university from 1957 to 1958, mostly from telephone exchange components, it was used primarily for educational purposes. It worked only until 1966, before being donated to another organisation.

The entire other side of the room is occupied by the enormous URAL-2 computer. The hall also includes many household appliances, radios and television sets – including the first Hungarian television set, the Orion AT-501 from 1955–56.

While Alan Turing helped the UK develop its first computer to break the Enigma code in the Second World War, and the US built ENIAC to calculate the trajectory of bullets, the Eastern Bloc was late with such developments. The URAL-2, designed and produced in the Soviet Union in 1962, worked via valves, or vacuum tubes. It was one of the first computers used in Hungary. Three versions were delivered to Hungary (this is the only remaining one), with access strictly limited to selected personnel. It had to be programmed directly (there was no programming language), and had no alphanumeric input or output. Its capacity of up to 12,000 floating-point calculations per second is below that of a modern pocket calculator.

Machinery related to movement is the theme of the third hall. The first section showcases water and air treatment technology, from pumps to compressors. The second highlights the steam era and the third focuses on engines. The world's first carburettor engine, invented in 1893 by Donát Bánki and János Csonka, is just one of the many treasures on show.

From the URAL-2 computer to Word and Excel development and a space mission

Charles Simonyi, the son of a Hungarian physicist, was lucky enough to have access to the URAL-2 computer as a boy. He later emigrated to the US, worked alongside Bill Gates on the development of Word and Excel software and became immensely rich. He also became the second Hungarian to leave Earth, on a short mission into space, taking one of the punched cards of the URAL-2 with him as a reminder of where he started.

KELENFÖLD POWER STATION

Art Deco meets early 20th-century technology

1116 Budapest, 60 Hengermalom út
Open for guided tours only (see Introduction) and on the Day of Power Plants in
October
Bus: 103, 133E – Hengermalom út

Designed in the 1920s and built mostly in the 1930s, the fantastic Kelenföld power station complex in southern Buda was a marvellous playground for urban exploration fans for years. It is now one of the very few major abandoned industrial sites which can officially be visited in Europe, along with the Óbuda Gas Works (see p. 154). Not all the factory is abandoned, though: Some buildings are empty and decaying, while other parts, which were restored between 2004 and 2008, are still operational.

Electricity came to Budapest in 1893 courtesy of two companies who ended up being bought in 1918 by the city municipality. The companies also initiated a project to build their own power station, the first beneficiaries of which were the 'Palatinus houses' near Margit Bridge, built at the same time.

The first buildings were designed by Kálmán Reichl, architect of the Óbuda Gas Works (1912–14), and built by the Ganz Electric Works and the Nicholson Machine Factory. Over the following decades, apart from during the First World War when development ceased, the site was extended. Following the death of Reichl in 1926, Virgil Borbíró (Bierbauer) took over his work. The first boiler room was built in 1913, the second in 1925, both designed by Reichl. The clock tower, dated 1926, was designed by Bierbauer – its size clearly illustrates how technology had advanced in the intervening years.

The brick-clad 30,000V switch house has a reinforced concrete structure and features a spectacular staircase on the façade. The bricks create harmony between the newer building and the older Reichl-designed ones.

The most spectacular area of the upper level is the control room. Reminiscent of early sci-fi films, it combines elements of modern and Art Deco styles. It is topped by a glass roof and has an abundance of switches and meters spanning the walls. Behind the switches, a corridor provides access to thousands of cables. The so-called 'relay hall' was situated on the lower level, with removable floor elements – again, providing easy access to the cables beneath. Glass flooring in the corridors permits natural light.

By 1934, the third boiler room was built. In parallel with the large housing projects being developed in the latter half of the 1960s, Kelenföld power station also began providing district heating (piped hot water).

The new power station introduced a new type of electricity, conforming to international standards: 3-phase, AC, 50Hz electricity with a system of transformers. The birth of the power station on 18 June 1914 was also the birthday of this modern electricity.

THE MAUSOLEUM OF THE TÖRLEY FAMILY

The crypt of the champagne makers

1221 Budapest, 6 Sarló utca
Guided tours only (see Introduction for operators), and check out local Péter-Pál days in June
budafokteteny.hu – website in Hungarian only
Bus: 241, 241A – Plébánia utca; Tram 47 – Leányka utcai lakótelep

A forgotten masterpiece of Hungarian Art Nouveau style, the partly renovated mausoleum of the famous champagne-maker family, the Törleys, lies on a hillside between the city centre and Budafok. It is one of the largest memorial buildings in Hungary that is not located in a cemetery.

Built in 1907–1909, the mausoleum was designed by Vilmos Rezső Ray, who also worked on the champagne factory and the castle of the Törley family. It is richly decorated in Art Nouveau style. Beneath the tower, stairs lead down to the crypt (where the earthly remains of several family members rested) which was vandalised in 1957. Today, the crypt is closed to visitors. Thanks to renovation work in 1996, the exterior of the building is in good condition, but its interiors clearly need larger scale renovation work. The rear entrance on the ground floor level leads to a chapel under the dome. Originally, it featured statues by József Damkó and stained-glass windows that were probably from the workshop of Miksa Róth. Unfortunately, the windows are gone, but remains of the decorative Art Nouveau wall paintings can still be seen. Just visible above the entrance of the chapel are the last remains of a beautiful mosaic.

József Törley: the founder of a champagne factory

After founding a champagne factory in 1882, József Törley was the largest champagne producer in the Austro-Hungarian Empire by the end of the century. In 1896 he was ennobled by Emperor Franz Joseph I. Following the death of József Törley in 1907, his widow ordered the construction of this mausoleum, located above the family castle.

THE ZSOLNAY ROOM

A wonderful example of Jugendstil

Törley factory
1221 Budapest, 7 Anna utca
torleymuzeum.hu/en, muzeum@torley.hu
See website for opening hours and guided tours
Tram: 47 – Savoyai Jenő tér
Bus 241 – Savoyai Jenő tér (Törley tér)

In addition to the mausoleum (see p. 204), there is another relic of the Törley family in Budafok: The Törley factory offers guided tours of its cellars, ending in the Zsolnay room, one side of which features a large

and beautiful wall of colourful tiles. The entire scene is a wonderful example of the Jugendstil style (German Art Nouveau). Created by Henrik Dařilek in the Zsolnay factory in 1904, the tile wall was restored in 1989. Glazed earthenware tiles in both gloss and matte finishes cover an area of 27 square metres.

Depicted on the tiles is the robed figure of József Törley: Seated at a stone table on the left, he welcomes a parade of brightly dressed guests entering from the right – one young boy carries a bowl of fruit, another carries a standard inscribed 'Törley sec'. The column on the right, wrapped in grape vines, bears the Törley family coat of arms, and beside it is the logo of the Zsolnay factory, the signature of Henrik Dařilek, and the year 1904.

THE BARREL OF LEANDERES CELLAR

One of the largest wine barrels in the world

14 Sörház utca, 1222 Budapest
bornegyed.hu
Individual visits: during events in August–September (like the Budafok
Champagne and Wine Festival in September) – see budafokteteny.hu and
bornegyed.hu
All year long, group visits can be arranged by email: marketing@torley.hu
Bus: 33, 114, 213, 214 – Vágóhíd utca: MÁV – Háros

In Budafok, once a wine region of Hungary, the Leanderes wine cellar hides a barrel that is among the largest in the world. With a capacity of 1,022 hectolitres (i.e. 102,200 litres, not 1,014 as indicated on a wooden plaque), it could provide a litre and a half of wine for every spectator in the 68,000-seater Ferenc Puskás Arena. Designed by István Borsody, the barrel was created in 1974 to mark the 25th anniversary of the state-owned Wine Production Company (*Boripari Vállalat*). The oak was selected from several regions of the country: 125 staves, each more than 6 metres long and 13-19 centimetres thick, were used in its construction. Its maximum diameter is 5.8 metres and it weighs 18 tonnes when empty: Unsurprisingly, it had to be assembled on site.

The head of the barrel is decorated with a wooden carving depicting a vine harvest scene, including travelling people making music for the celebration. In the centre is a banner bearing a quote from a Hungarian poem by Ferenc Kölcsey: 'Look to the future and measure the present by what you wish to achieve / Do, create, enrich, and the country will arise'. The carving was created by István Szabó, who also appears in the image as the character checking the quality of the wine.

Among others, the internationally renowned Irsai Olivér wine is produced in this cellar under the Szent István Korona brand.

The largest in Central Eastern Europe, stretching for almost 100 kilometres, the cellar system of Budafok has been in use for more than three centuries. As a result of limestone mining, 6 to 8 metre-wide and 3 to 4 metre-high mineshafts were created. Around 10 per cent of Hungary's white wine is stored here. In the best cellars, the temperature variation is just 1 to 2 degrees Celsius, with a constant temperature of 12 to 14 degrees throughout the year.

The world's largest wine barrel has been in Heidelberg Castle, Germany, since 1751. With a capacity of 228,000 litres, it is one of the leading tourist attractions, though it is no longer filled with wine.

THE CAVE DWELLERS
OF BUDAFOK

Life in an apartment carved from stone

1222 Budapest, 4 Veréb utca
+36 (20) 447 8333 (In Hungarian only)
budafokibarlanglakas.hu
Call ahead to make an appointment, open from 1 March to 31 October
Bus: 141 – Széchenyi utca or 58, 158, 250, 250B – Mező utca

In a remote little street in the 22nd district of Budapest, the last cave dwellings of Budafok (formerly known as Promontor) offer an insight into a poor but unique way of living. They are preserved here, complete with furniture and constant high humidity.

These dwellings were carved directly from Promontor limestone: Their low-level yards were dug from the surface, and the stone that was removed was used for construction in Budapest, particularly after the devastating 1838 flood. Small 'apartments' with two to three rooms were then carved into the walls.

Sometimes natural caves were found and became inhabited, the longest one being 160 metres in length. As no walls or roofs needed to be built (only a door, a chimney and a few windows), construction costs were low.

However, these flats remained humid and dark throughout the year. A humidity sensor in one of the rooms clearly indicates this: It always shows 100 per cent humidity. Anything made of wood, paper or iron eventually rusts and decays.

An article from 1912 described the area's miserable conditions: Heavy rainfall resulted in damp walls, there was a lack of lighting in the muddy streets, and cholera and TB were rife among the hundreds of poor tenants, mostly agricultural and industrial workers.

Even though the creation of these cave dwellings was prohibited in 1910, new ones kept appearing. The last tenants moved out as late as the 1960s. After that, most of the yards were filled in or reused for wine storage or mushroom cultivation. The Veréb utca site is the only remaining example.

THE ROSARIUM IN BUDATÉTÉNY

A must-see for garden lovers

1223 Budapest, 188 Nagytétényi út
The garden also hosts occasional concerts, fairs and shows
For the events, visit facebook.com/BudatetenyiRozsakert
Every day, 8am–8pm
Bus: 138, 150 – Budatétény vasútállomás (Campona); MÁV – Budatétény station

If you are a fan of roses and gardens, this remote but large rose garden will be a feast for your eyes. It is the largest of its kind in Hungary, with thousands of varieties planted.

From the Buda side, head south towards Nagytétényi út to reach the 22nd district of Budapest and enter through the main gate at 188 Nagytétényi út.

It is advisable to set aside a few hours for a visit. The garden is spread across two and a half acres, split into nine zones, with around 10,000 square metres dedicated to rose beds. More than 7,000 roses are grown.

The main purpose of the rosarium is preservation. There are many

older varieties that can no longer be bought in nurseries, so the garden performs a vital role as a gene bank, conducting important scientific research.

The garden began in 1950 when the Horticultural Research Institute was established. Gergely Márk was the most active collector of roses in Hungary, with more than 200 varieties in the garden supplied by him. This first garden was planted around the György Mansion in Budatétény, but soon proved too small. Between 1964 and 1965 the garden was moved to the current location. It was originally much larger but was later reduced in size due to construction and the sale of some of the land, affecting mostly those species not resistant to winter frost. A partial reconstruction began from 1993–95 as part of Budapest's bid to host the World Expo.

Information tables help identify varieties. In the upper left corner, Roman numerals show the larger zone, followed by a number identifying the exact location. On the right, a registration number identifies the specific item. With so many varieties, several roses may bear the same name, so the registration number is essential to keep track of them.

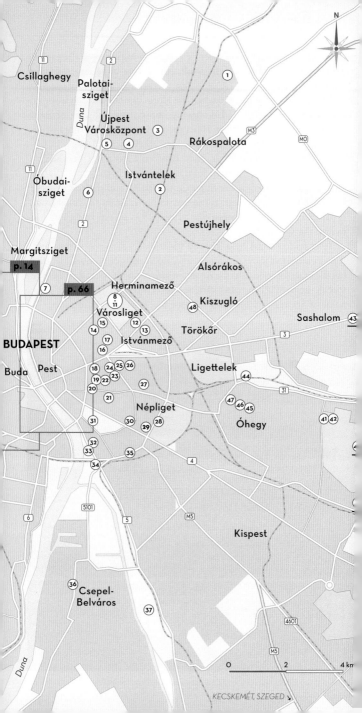

Pest

MUNICIPAL WASTE RECYCLING FACILITY

A truly spectacular visit

1151 Budapest, 10-12 Mélyfúró utca
fkf.hu/letesitmeny-latogatas
Guided tour groups only (see website)
Bus: 125 – Hulladékhasznosító mű

Built between 1977 and 1981 (although the company that owns it dates back to 1895), the Municipal Waste Recycling Facility and its 120 metre-high chimney at the end of Mélyfúró utca can be visited on guided tours. It is a truly spectacular experience, not to be missed.

Nearly 60 percent of the city's waste – more than 400,000 tonnes every year – is brought here for incineration, which then produces heat and electricity for the public. During the guided tours, visitors can see the whole process: the emptying of trucks, the claw grabber that can lift five tonnes of waste, furnaces, the control room, and the treatment of waste and smoke.

The space also includes a small museum (opened in 1985) that showcases all kinds of objects related to the company's operation: waste transportation and watercarts, early non-motorised tools, and an old waste bin. One of the oldest pieces is a Rába water-cart with wooden wheels that was in use from the 1910s. The operator, sitting in the rear, would communicate with the driver via a mouthpiece. The most specialised vehicle is the one that is still used to clean the Buda Castle Tunnel.

ISTVÁNTELEK

The post-apocalyptic atmosphere of a train cemetery

1045 Budapest, 5–7 Elem utca
mavrailtours.hu
Guided tours only (see website)
Train: MÁV – Istvántelek; Bus 121 – Istvántelki út/Elem utca

Once a major base for the maintenance of railway vehicles, the large site of the Hungarian State Railways in Istvántelek, in the 4th district of Budapest, resembles a cemetery of steam locomotives and old carriages. Its unique, almost post-apocalyptic atmosphere attracts many 'illegal' urban explorers and guided tour visitors.

To the annoyance of the locals, as the city expanded, Nyugati railway station became busier and busier. By the end of the 19th century, locals were fed up with the smoke and noise of steam trains. The relatively small area was inadequate for carrying out vital maintenance, so the situation had to be resolved, and service functions were moved to a larger site in Istvántelek, where construction began in 1901. The Nyugati station remained in its original location.

By 1902, a maintenance hall for carriages was built, followed a year later by a similar hall for locomotives. It was fully opened on 1 June 1904.

During the communist era, the site was named after Jenő Landler, a communist politician and director of the state railways. It was closed in 1992, with only a small section remaining in operation for warehousing and maintenance. The two water towers, one of which can be visited, were renovated by 2011.

Unfortunately, the roof of the carriage maintenance hall is in such poor condition that entry is now strictly forbidden. But visitors are allowed in the locomotive maintenance hall, where some minor repairs are still carried out for small-gauge railways or for the Museum of Transportation. Vehicles stored there include a 301 Class locomotive, the largest of its era, a 424 Class Hungarian locomotive with a huge red star on its front, postal carriages, specialised vehicles such as a locomotive with a flamethrower on the front to combat frost and snow, a 'smiling' carriage designed for use on the Children's Railway (see p.166), a fire-free steam locomotive that was filled with steam only, so it could enter a factory producing alcoholic drinks and dozens of other vintage wonders.

THE BUTTERFLY MUSEUM

Thousands of insects and other exotic relics packed into a house

1041 Budapest, 26 Dessewffy utca - Újpest
ujpestilepkemuzeum.hu
Tue–Fri 10am–4pm, Sat–Sun 10am–5pm, guided tours available
Tram: 12, 14 - Szülőotthon; Bus: 96 – Szülőotthon or 20E, 96, 220 – Újpesti rendelőintézet

One of the smallest in Hungary, occupying just a single room, the Butterfly Museum in Újpest houses more than 2,000 objects in its collection.

Opened in 2003, it was founded by György Juhász (1945–2015) who spent four decades travelling the world, collecting not only butterflies and other insects, but also periwinkles, shells, fossils and minerals, along with cultural artefacts, photographs and other interesting items. The collection is truly global, featuring items from places as far flung as Papua New Guinea, Israel, Bolivia, India, the Venezuelan rain forests, and the deserts of Africa.

Welcoming visitors to the museum is the largest object in the collection: the skeleton of a bear… but the butterflies are definitely the main attraction. The incredible range of species provides a wonderful insight into the intense colours and patterns present in nature. The wings of one are lilac from one angle, but yellow from another. Males are usually more brightly coloured than females and butterflies that are active during the day are generally brighter than more nocturnal varieties.

Only about a fifth of the entire collection is on display, partly due to the lack of space, partly because some butterflies, such as the *Victoria*, need to be protected from light. In total, 179 butterfly species are registered in the Carpathian basin – each one can be found in the museum's collection.

Truly unique among the other insect specimens on display is the reproduction method of the ichneumon fly, more commonly known as the Darwin wasp. The female lays its eggs in the body of a tarantula (or other prey) and the eggs hatch into carnivorous larvae that eat their host. It was this reproduction method that inspired the creators of the *Alien* horror movies.

The light refracting qualities of some butterfly wings is so specialised that they were even once used as a security element on US bank notes.

THE SOCIALIST COAT OF ARMS OF BUDAPEST

A symbol has survived the last three decades

Újpest Town Hall
1041 Budapest, 14 István út
Metro: M3 – Újpest-Központ

It may look strange, but decades after the end of the socialist era, the town hall of Újpest – the 4th district of Budapest – is still decorated with the pre-1990 coat of arms of Budapest, with a red star in its centre. It is on the front façade, under the tower on the right-hand side.

Újpest was an independent town before the creation of today's 'Great Budapest' in 1950. At the end of the 19th century, as the town's population had been increasing, a new town hall building was needed. The 1898 design competition was won by architects Henrik Böhm and Ármin Hegedűs, and the town hall was built very quickly. It opened in 1900, and as well as giving home to the municipality of Újpest, it included a law court and a prison. The façade features Art Nouveau decorations carved in stone, delicate brick layering, and is topped by a statue of Roland, the legendary Frankish hero who fought under Charlemagne.

The building was 'upgraded' with the socialist coat of arms of Budapest following the creation of 'Great Budapest' in 1950, replacing the coat of arms of the Károlyi family, the founders of Újpest. After 1990, these socialist symbols (decorations on buildings, red stars, statues etc.) were usually removed from the streets of Budapest. However, for unknown reasons, the town hall of Újpest kept this old coat of arms.

A mysterious clock

A mysterious element of the façade is the clock in the middle. The architectural plans dating from 1898 show a real clock, but when the building was completed in 1900, a working clock had not been placed there. Instead, a clock was sculpted with mysterious letter combinations: CsL, FT, MJ and BL at the quarter points, and HJ in the middle. So far, no historian has been able to find out the meaning.

Further vestiges from the socialist era

– The station buildings of the Children's Railway (see p. 166)
– The gateway of 3 Széll Kálmán tér with a mosaic tile image that commemorates the old name of the square, Moszkva tér (Moscow square). Depicting the Red Square and the Kremlin, the mosaic (100 x 80 cm) was placed here in 1952 following the renaming of the square from Széll Kálmán tér to Moszkva tér in November 1951
– A mural made of metal on the wall of MOM Cultural Center can be seen on the front façade of the building on the pedestrian promenade side. It features an industrial chimney, a tractor, workers, a hammer and sickle and a harvest scene – all communist themes
– A street sign on the corner of Vámház körút and Királyi Pál utca reads '*Tolbuchin körút*' (after Fedor Ivanovich Tolbukhin, a military commander and Marshal of the Soviet Union)

STATUE OF THE WARRIOR OF THE HUNGARIAN RED ARMY

A reminder of the Hungarian Soviet Republic, a short-lived communist dictatorship in 1919

1042 Budapest, Szabadság Park
Metro: M3 – Újpest-Városkapu

In front of Szabadság Park, the statue of the Warrior of the Hungarian Red Army is not really a secret with its 2.5-metre figure on a 4-metre pedestal. Few, however, know what it represents. Unveiled on 21 March 1959, it commemorates the 40th anniversary of the declaration of the short-lived Hungarian Soviet Republic (see opposite page).

The sculptor of the statue was Tamás Gyenes (1920–1963), a favoured artist of his era, while the base was designed by József Schall (1913–89). The figure depicts a warrior worker of the Red Army stepping forward, holding his gun up high. The pedestal once bore the inscription *MAGYAR VÖRÖSHADSEREG HARCOSA* (WARRIOR OF THE RED ARMY), but it is no longer there. After 1990, many communist statues and memorials were removed from the streets of Budapest. However, in this case historians claimed that the warriors of the Red Army were fighting for their country, and many of them remained soldiers after the fall of the Hungarian Soviet Republic, so their service to the nation was deemed more important than the fact that they served in the Red Army. Hence, this statue became an exception: It was not destroyed nor relocated.

What was the Hungarian Soviet Republic of 1919?

The Hungarian Council Republic, also called the Hungarian Soviet Republic, was the short-lived political regime in Hungary from 21 March to 6 August 1919. This regime was the second communist government in history after that of Soviet Russia was established in 1917. Its main leader was Béla Kun, officially in charge of Foreign Affairs. It lasted only 133 days and collapsed when French, Romanian, Serbian and nationalist forces, supported by the French mission commanded by Henri Berthelot, occupied Budapest on 6 August 1919. On 16 November 1918, the Hungarian Democratic Republic had been proclaimed, putting an end to the monarchy in Hungary and definitively severing ties between Hungary and the former Austro-Hungarian Empire of the Habsburg-Lorraine dynasty. The republic was proclaimed by Count Mihály Károlyi who became the head of the government. That same month of November, the Communist Party of Hungary was founded by the merger of several distinct groups, with Béla Kun, returning from Moscow with an informal mandate from Lenin, taking effective leadership. After the First World War, deep nationalist discontent arose from the considerable losses of territory imposed at the end of the war. The country was in complete disarray, the situation having led to millions of Hungarians in unemployment or poverty, and a significant part of the population was sensitive to communist propaganda. On 20 March 1919, following a request for yet another territorial surrender, Mihály Károlyi resigned. Quickly, a note circulated, supposedly signed by him, announcing that he was 'transmitting power to the proletariat'. The Communist Party, allied with the Social Democratic Party, took power. While the Russian Soviet Republic, occupied by the civil war on its soil, was not able to come to its aid, communist Hungary nevertheless wished to recover its lost territories and quickly entered into conflict with all the neighbouring countries. In April, Czechoslovak troops attacked communist Hungary to prevent it from taking over the territory of former Upper Hungary, whose inhabitants were predominantly Slovaks. An attack by Hungarian troops against the Romanian army (July 17–20) had disastrous consequences: The Franco-Romanian forces broke through the Hungarian positions and entered Budapest on 6 August 1919, marking the end of the Soviet regime in Budapest.

MOSAICS OF THE FORMER DISINFECTION INSTITUTE

An old centre for the treatment of infectious diseases

1138 Budapest, 174 Váci út
Metro: M3 – Gyöngyösi utca

Not far from Gyöngyösi utca station, the Disinfection Institute was designed in the early 20th century by Dezső Hönig. Best viewed from over the road, the beautiful facade features decorative brickwork interspersed with very nicely designed mosaics and a large section reading 'Fertőtlenítő Intézet' (Disinfection Institute).

The old institute used to treat patients infected by plague, cholera, pox and rash typhus. After disinfection, re-entry to the infected side was strictly forbidden to patients and staff. The work was indeed risky, and

several workers died there in the 1910s and 1920s.

The large chimney in the yard was connected to a furnace for burning rubbish and the dung of infected animals.

The clean side included offices, workshops, garages, stables, the boiler room, a staff kitchen and dining room. There were also apartments for the director and some staff members, along with rooms for training purposes.

The southern half of the structure was the 'infected' side, the northern the 'clean' side, and disinfection took place in between. People were bathed and treated while their belongings (clothes, furniture and mattresses) were disinfected in large chambers using steam and formalin.

The chambers are still inside, but no longer in use.

Today, the institute is called the National Public Health Institute of the Central Hungarian Region. It provides, among other things, vaccinations for those travelling to exotic countries.

STAIRWAY OF
38-40 POZSONYI ÚT

⑦

The luxury of the 1930s revisited

1137 Budapest, Pozsonyi út
Guided tours available, see introduction for operators
Trolley Bus: 75, 76 – Szent István park

The district that lies north of the Pest end of Margit bridge (called Újlipótváros) underwent a short period of rapid development in the early 1930s, resulting in the construction of, among other things, magnificent staircases, leading to the apartments of the rich and famous of the era. A tax incentive even encouraged investors to complete buildings as quickly as possible, so most were built with a reinforced concrete structure. A perimetric approach was obligatory on most plots, buildings had to be 25 metres high, and façades uniformly shaped. The intensive development was alleviated by the creation of Szent István Park, around which are some of the area's most desirable places to live, thanks in part to the splendid staircases and foyers.

One of the finest examples can be found at 38-40 Pozsonyi út. Built by the Hatvany family, who owned Alföldi Sugar Factory Inc., its architects were Béla Hofstätter and Ferenc Domány, who also worked together on several other blocks in the area. The ground floor has always been a café (also worth a visit for its beautifully restored interiors). At the entrance, the marble benches, nameplates and in-house telephone system were all designed to reflect the high status of the tenants. Services also

included a concierge, elevators, a pram storage room and a ventilation system bringing in fresh air from the Danube. Two staircases lead to a roof terrace. The spiral staircases are clad in marble, with blue 'Emergé' rubber inserts in the middle.

NEARBY

42 Pozsonyi út

Designed and built in harmony with 38-40 (Hofstätter and Domány again), the interior of this building features marble clad walls, a glass stairway, Emergé rubber flooring inserts, and circular nameplates which are all still visible today. The investor was the agricultural company Hungarian Rabbethge and Giesecke Seed Culture Inc.

44-46 Pozsonyi út

Built in 1935-36, this apartment building was designed by Béla Málnai. The investor company was the Pension Institute of Hungarian General Coal Mines. The upper levels have an H-shaped layout, creating two inner yards. In one, a large plant holder is decorated with the relief of a miner.

THE DRAGONS OF CITY PARK

Former 'icebreakers' of the Chain Bridge

City Park (Városliget)1146 Budapest, Városliget
Metro: M1 –Széchenyi fürdő

When visiting the zoo at the northern end of City Park (Városliget), you can see two large cast iron dragons, each painted green. The dragons' eyes show power and strength, their mouths snarl menacingly, their tails are S-shaped, and their teeth are sharp.

Cast in the famous iron foundry of Ignác Schlick in 1856, they were part of a group of three dragon statues that were originally located at the Pest end of the Chain Bridge, the first loading dock in the capital city where they served as icebreakers.

When the quay was reconstructed, the dragons were first moved to the City Park.

Finally, two of them ended up in the zoo, while a third one is guarding the entrance of the Kiscelli Museum.

THE BUST OF BÉLA LUGOSI ⑨

Installed secretly in the dead of night ...

City Park (Városliget)1146 Budapest, Városliget
Metro: M1 – Hősök tere or Széchenyi fürdő

In the south-east corner of the rear side of Vajdahunyad castle is a bust of Béla Lugosi (1882–1956), the Hungarian-American actor, best known for playing Count Dracula in the 1924 Broadway play and its 1931 film version. The bust is supported by a small figure of a devil that reminds us of what made him famous. Strangely enough, the bust was not installed by the city but just 'appeared' secretly on the night of 19 July 2003 at around 10 o'clock. For more than a decade, even its sculptor remained anonymous, the only clue being two engraved letters on the stone: HZ. They refer to the sculptor, German graphic artist and musician Hartmut Zech. He and his friends installed the statue silently in the dead of night, just like Dracula ...

Buried wearing one of the Dracula costume capes

Born Béla Ferenc Dezső Blaskó, Béla Lugosi took the name Lugosi in 1903 to honour his birthplace, Lugos (now Lugoj in Romania). He became world famous for playing the character of Count Dracula, and was restricted to Dracula and 'mad scientist' roles due to his strong Hungarian accent. He died of a heart attack in 1956 in Los Angeles, aged 73. At the request of his son Béla G. Lugosi and fourth wife Lillian, he was buried wearing one of the Dracula costume capes.

THE 'FUIT' GRAVE

A reference to an 1877 poem

City Park (Városliget)1146 Budapest, Városliget
Metro: M1 – Hősök tere or Széchenyi fürdő

In City Park, in the area between Ajtósi Dürer sor and Zichy Mihály út, a mysterious stone obelisk bears the word 'Fuit' ('was' in Latin). Although this simple word on a grave, with no name, gave birth to several legends (some say it is the grave of a Hungarian poet with a broken heart or of a Hungarian aristocrat who committed suicide), it is actually the grave of Jakab Horváth, the advocate who defended Martinovics during his trial.

In his last will and testament, Horváth asked to be buried in City

Park. The word 'Fuit' refers to an 1877 poem by János Arany *Ének a Pesti Ligetről* ('Song of the City Park'), which ends with the lines (roughly translated) '…Your name is only what a tombstone in this grove reads, Fuit.'

Horváth died in 1806 (not in 1809 as the stone indicates). The grave was completely rebuilt in 1928, and in 1995 the fence was put up.

A short description (in Hungarian) can also be read on the back of the stone. Every year on Easter Sunday, local civic organisations bring flowers to the grave, opening the summer season of the park.

FORMER M1 METRO BRIDGE

⑪

A bridge to nowhere

City Park (Városliget)1146 Budapest, Városliget
Metro: M1 – Hősök tere or Széchenyi fürdő

In the area between Heroes' Square and the lake, a small red and white bridge appears mysteriously, spanning only a flat area of grass.

When it was originally built, today's M1 metro line came above ground after Heroes' Square and terminated near the zoo and Széchenyi Baths (see p. 189 for an old photo taken from this bridge).

Designed by Róbert Wünsch, the bridge was built as an overpass above the tracks.

However, when Budapest celebrated its centenary in 1973, the M1 line was extended to Mexikói út: The old terminus became unused and the tracks were removed, making the bridge redundant.

Built in 1896, the bridge is one of the earliest reinforced concrete bridges in Hungary and has been kept as protected heritage.

STATUE OF A WOMAN

A bride turned to stone

1146 Budapest, 61 Thököly út
Bus: 5, 7, 110, 112 – Stefánia út / Thököly út

I f you look closely at the balcony of the house at 61 Thököly út, you will notice a mysterious bust of a woman.

Built in 1912 by sewing machine merchant Manó Pápai for his daughter Irén and her solicitor husband Dr. Jenő Preszler, the house was designed by architect Lajos Ybl, a relative of Miklós Ybl.

Lajos Ybl's son Ervin studied in France, where he saw the palace of Jacques Coeur in Bourges, the entrance of which is watched by two stone figures. Ervin showed photographs of the figures to his father, who then proposed a similar statue for the new villa in Thököly út. The Pápai family liked the idea and asked Miklós Ligeti to be the sculptor.

During the past century, the mysterious woman gave rise to several stories. One journalist wrote that the woman's husband was sent to war and that she used to wait for hours on the balcony for news about him. When she was informed that her husband had been killed, the woman died on the balcony.

In another version, the news of the death turned out to be false, and the returning husband raised the statue in memory of the woman.

According to another version given by writer Milán Füst, the woman waved to her husband from this balcony as he took the tram to work every morning. When she died, the husband raised the statue in her memory.

> The best time to see the statue is in the spring or autumn when it is not obscured by leaves.

THE ROOF AND DECORATIONS OF THE GEOLOGICAL AND GEOPHYSICAL INSTITUTE

Art Nouveau in blue

1143 Budapest, 14 Stefánia út
Free access to the entrance hall
Full interior visit: European Heritage Days in September
Trolley Bus: 75 – Egressy út / Stefánia út

Built between 1898 and 1900 by architect Ödön Lechner using a mix of Art Nouveau and traditional Hungarian folk art styles, the stunning Geological and Geophysical Institute boasts, among other beauties, a stunning roof entirely tiled in varying shades of blue and turquoise, blending almost seamlessly with the sky. The tiles were originally produced in the renowned Zsolnay factory.

Perched at the very top of the roof, four seated Atlas figures support a globe on their shoulders. The surfaces and windows of the façade are also outlined in brick, and feature inlaid ceramics in a similarly vibrant blue. The floral patterns were inspired by Transylvanian folk architecture and the decorative patterns of József Huszka in the 1880s.

This gorgeous building stands close to the Institute for the Blind: To the right of the main entrance gate, integrated into the bricks, are small, tactile ceramic plates that enable visually impaired people to also experience Lechner's work. In the entrance hall (free access), the flowing patterns and the arches of the walls and windows create the impression of a cave, decorated with colourful paintings. Other parts of the interior, including a small exhibit about Hungary's geology, can be visited during the European Heritage Days which take place in September.

THE CALVINIST CHURCH
ON VÁROSLIGETI FASOR

A splendid mix of architectural styles

1071 Budapest, 5 Városligeti fasor
fasor.hu (check for upcoming events)
Open before the 10am Sunday service
Metro: M1 – Kodály Körönd

Built in 1913 by the architect Aladár Árkay (known as the architect of Budai Vigado, together with Mór Kallina, and of the St Gellért memorial on Gellért Hill), the out of the ordinary Calvinist church at 5 Városligeti fasor is a splendid mix of architectural styles: Finnish and Transylvanian folk architecture, the British Arts and Crafts movement and Otto Wagner's interiors.

Wealthy jeweller Adolf Laky, who also took part in the renovation of the royal crown, donated 300,000 koronas to the construction.

The robust bell tower and main façade are accented by pairs of small windows. Surrounding the wide arch of the front entrance are dozens of majolica tiles, all produced in the Zsolnay factory. The ceramics and interior decoration are based on traditional Hungarian folk patterns and can be seen as forerunners of Art Deco. Árkay designed not only the exterior of the building in the Art Nouveau style, but also the interior, including the lighting, the benches, the patterns of the wall decorations and the stained glass windows. The windows were produced by the most famous

glass and ceramics artist of the era, Miksa Róth.

The layout of the church resembles a cross, with a wide dome spanning its centre. On three sides are multi-storey galleries, while the pulpit takes centre stage. Originally, the church was designed with its tower on the opposite side. However, the director of the neighbouring Herczel Surgical Sanatorium convinced the architect to alter the layout, moving the tower to its present position.

Miksa Róth (1865-1944) followed his father into the profession of glassmaking, eventually setting up his own business in 1885. He created not only glass works, but from 1897, also ceramics. Róth created the largest mosaic tile in Budapest, found in Szervita tér. Influenced by historical styles as well as Art Nouveau and Art Deco, his works decorate many famous buildings in Budapest and elsewhere: The Parliament House, Gresham Palace and the Liszt Academy of Music, among others. The Hungarian National Archives in the Castle District also feature Róth's artworks.

WINNIE-THE-POOH MINI STATUE ⑮

The house where the translator of Winnie the Pooh was born

27 Damjanich utca
Trolley Bus 70 – Nefelejcs utca

On the façade of 27 Damjanich utca, a mini statue of Winnie-the-Pooh can be spotted. The reason for the bear figure appearing here is that Milne's famous novel was translated to Hungarian by writer, poet and translator Frigyes Karinthy, who was born in this house in 1887 (see p. 28).

THE FOYER OF THE PÉTERFY SÁNDOR UTCA HOSPITAL AND HEALTH CENTRE

Luxury healthcare since the 1930s

1076 Budapest, 8-20 Péterfy Sándor utca
Weekdays 7am–7pm
Trolleybus: 73, 76, 79 – Péterfy Sándor utca

The modern glass foyer of the Péterfy Sándor utca Hospital and Health Centre is a beautiful construction, typical of 1930s style and functionality, but little known except to people using the hospital. The architect Dr Dezső Hültl designed all parts of the building for practicality: His priority was to achieve a logical layout for the doctors' offices and other departments, so the thousands of people using the building could navigate it efficiently. Though of lesser importance, the aesthetics of the design were clearly not ignored: Dezső Hültl won the master prize of the Association of Hungarian Architects for the construction of this building. The foyer was considered a work of art due to the architectonic arrangement of the staircases and the use of noble stone cladding.

Construction began in 1932, and by 1943, along with the main structure, the adjacent buildings were also erected. Between 1929 and 1949 it was operated by MABI (Magánalkalmazottak Biztosító Intézete – Insurance Institute for the Privately Employed). The lower three levels of the building were built for the health centre, and the upper levels for the hospital.

Two sections of the foyer roof were built on sliding rails so they could be opened in summer for ventilation, and heated in winter to prevent snow covering the roof. The 'Luxfer' ceiling glass was produced by Haas and Somogyi, a renowned company of the time.

NEARBY

Noah's Arc mini statue ⑰

In the proximity of the hospital, a mini statue by Mihály Kolodko (see p. 28) can be visited. Located by the playground in Bethlen Gábor tér, it shows Noah's Arc. The choice of the Old Testament story of the savior of animals can be explained by the institutions in the area: a status quo synagogue and the University of Veterinary Medicine.

THE MOSAICS IN NÉPSZÍNHÁZ UTCA

The largest mosaic in Budapest, depicting the heavenly origin of beer

1081 Budapest, 22 Népszínház utca
Metro: M4 – II. János Pál pápa tér; Tram: 28, 28A, 37, 37A – II. János Pál pápa tér

Just beneath the overhanging roof of 22 Népszínház utca, about halfway between Blaha Lujza tér and II. János Pál pápa tér, the beautiful mosaics that cover roughly 60 square metres form the largest mosaic in the city – the three mosaic panels depict the heavenly origin of

beer. In the middle, Gambrinus, the king of lager beer, is arriving with barrels on a carriage pulled by white horses. Crowds are gathering from either side and the foamy brew is flowing towards them. The decorative carvings on the façade below include barley and hops, key ingredients of beer production.

The house was built in 1906 by Polgári Serfőzde, one of the large breweries that once operated in Budapest (architect Emil Vidor also designed factory buildings for the brewery). Celebrating beer, the mosaic is one of the lesser-known works of Miska Róth, who also worked with painter Andor Dudits.

The latest restoration works on the mosaic were completed in 2019. Many of the tiles had to be reproduced individually, as the range of tiles available today is not nearly as wide as that available to Róth more than a century ago. Some of the tiles were even imported from Venice.

MARTSA STUDIOS

A small and very charming artists' colony

1084 Budapest, 37 József utca
martsamuterem@gmail.com
martsamuterem.hu
Appointments via email, or check the events of European Heritage Days in
September
Tram: 4, 6 – Harminckettesek tere; Bus: 9 – Muzsikus cigányok parkja or 99 –
Mátyás tér

In a charming hidden back yard, the Martsa studios have been home to artists since 1901. They include a workshop, an artist's studio and a lovely little garden that can be visited by appointment. The first artist to move in was sculptor Géza Maróti, best known for his work on public buildings. Dozens more painters, photographers and sculptors have worked here from time to time, including architect Károly Kós, who probably designed the Budapest Zoo pavilions here.

In 1949 sculptor István Martsa moved in. It was his wife, Ilona M Szűcs, who researched and published the history of the site and of the businesses that once operated here. Thanks to her, the building became a protected heritage site in 2011. Today, the Martsa family still maintains the studios and backyard.

The site was first occupied by Béla Seenger, who, assisted by local craftsmen, provided carved stones for many building projects in Budapest. In 1876 he purchased the site at 6 Tavaszmező utca and moved his business there. Three years later he purchased the plot at 37 József utca and built another stone carving workshop. The house on the street front was erected in 1899. Seenger supplied carved stones for the Opera, many buildings on Andrássy út, and for the interior of the Parliament building, to name just a few. At the beginning of the 20th century, Seenger moved his business to Buda.

On the wall of the first studio building are stones marking the grants given to the valiants of Miklós Horthy in the 1930s. Horthy was the country's head of state until 1944; valiants, or knights, were men awarded the Vitéz order of merit. Originally, the stones were coloured; Those displayed here are faulty. Discovered in 2010, they were initially intended to be incorporated into a pavement. Many bear the marks of their maker.

The garden is adorned with several gypsum copies of István Martsa's statues. The original *Showering Woman* can be seen at the railway station in Siófok, while the original *Sitting Woman* is in the garden of Füvészkert. The two large rooms that used to be the workshops of István Martsa and Ilona M Szűcs are now used as an exhibition area and workshop for the family's works.

THE STAIRCASE OF
THE KOZMO HOTEL

The largest staircase in the city

Former József Telephone Exchange, 1082 Budapest, Horváth Mihály tér
Bus: 9 – Horváth Mihály tér; Trolley Bus: 72, 83 – Horváth Mihály tér

Housed in the former József Telephone Exchange, the Kozmo luxury hotel boasts two beautiful features: a stunning staircase that some hotel guests don't even notice if they only take the lift, and beautiful outside reliefs on the façade that reflect its past. Designed by architect

© zsoltbatar

Rezső Vilmos Ray, with a reinforced concrete structure by Szilárd Zielinszky, the József Telephone Exchange was built in 1915.

At the heart of the building, the single flight stairs are 11 metres wide and 50 metres in length, making it larger than the main staircase of the Parliament. The reason for this size is that for the distribution of calls, network plugs had to be connected manually on switchboards. The two large exchange halls (where connections were handled semi-automatically, mostly by female staff) were surrounded by an enormous number of wires and cables, making it a hazardous workplace for fire safety. The wide staircase therefore formed a quick escape route for the employees in case of fire.

A picturesque façade

On the right-hand side of the building are four reliefs depicting postal and communication services: a pigeon with an envelope in its claws; a winged iron wheel with a horn above it, symbolising the cooperation between the postal and rail services; a horn beneath the royal crown; and a serpent coiled around a postbox.

Above the main gate, a child holds a horn in one hand and a small globe in the other; the sculptor Ignác Langer perhaps imagined a young Hermes. Nearby, an angel holds a telephone transmitter, while at the corner are portraits of Tivadar Puskás and Ferenc Puskás: Tivadar invented the telephone exchange and set up Telefon Hírmondó, a 'telephone news service', while his brother Ferenc established the first telephone exchange in Budapest. At ground level, the cladding features a large relief sculpted by István Damkó between 1912 and 1913: an allegorical depiction of communication, including early electricity posts. On the Német utca side, the reliefs between the windows show a rectangular object: CB I, one of the earliest telephone appliances in the city.

NEARBY

Meerkat mini statue

The fence of 53-54 Bókay János utca has a unique feature: You can spot a tiny statue on it (see p. 128) It depicts a cute-looking meerkat. The sculptor, Mihály Kolodko, chose this animal to draw attention to a foundation called the Meerkat Foundation for Children with Diabetes, working in the Childrens' Hospital that is found here. The opportunity for the creation of this mini statue was the 100th anniversary of the invention of insulin in 1922.

JÓZSEF ERNYEY LIBRARY AND SAINT CHRISTIAN PHARMACY

One of the city's oldest pharmacies, hidden behind shutters

1084 Budapest, 3 Mátyás tér
semmelweismuseum.hu
Visits by prior arrangement (see website) or during the Day of Pharmacies
events (June)
Bus: 99 – Mátyás tér

The shutters of the large shop windows are invariably closed, making it difficult to discover what is behind. But the ground floor of 3 Mátyás tér, in the heart of the 8th district, conceals a historic pharmacy, one of the oldest in Budapest.

It's also home to a pharmaceutical library.

The building was commissioned by János Filó (1852-1917), an outstanding figure in Hungarian pharmaceutical circles, and a chemist of the St Christian (Szt. Keresztély) Pharmacy.

A carving of the saint can be seen inside, flanked by portraits of two Greek mythological figures: Asclepius (the god of medicine) and Hygieia (his daughter, goddess of health, cleanliness and hygiene). The Neo-Renaissance oak interiors, protected since 1958, are original and as old as the building itself. The carpentry was by Lajos Valnicsek, whose beautiful shelves are packed with vintage porcelain and glass storage vessels.

The pharmacy was opened in the neighbouring building on 5 March 1882 and relocated here on 8 November 1890. Later additions include an office, laboratory, storage room, a bandage factory, and apartments for the pharmacist and his assistant.

An interesting feature of the adjacent office is the in-house telephone by the pharmacist's desk, which was connected to the apartments, the laboratory, the factory and the kitchen. The pharmacy operated here until 1978; Following a com-

plete renovation, it reopened as an exhibition and library reading room in 1981.

The collecting of relics from the history of Hungarian pharmacy was begun by (among others) József Ernyey in 1896.

In 1906 he founded the pharmaceutical history collection of the Hungarian Chemists' Association. The collection in the library here is based on his work.

THE JEWISH HOUSE OF PRAYER IN TELEKI TÉR

The last remnant of more than 40 Jewish houses of prayer

1086 Budapest, 22 Teleki László tér
budapestshul.com
info@telekiter.com
Open on Saturday mornings, arrive by 8:30am
Tram: 28, 28A, 37, 37A – Teleki László tér or 24 – Dologház utca

More than forty small Jewish houses of prayer once stood in the 8th district of Budapest (Lujza utca, Dobozi utca, Erdélyi utca, etc.), as well as kosher food stores and cafes. The mother of world-famous photographer André Kertész even had a kosher coffee store at 6 Teleki tér. After the Holocaust, most prayer houses in Budapest closed down. The last one still operating is at 22 Teleki tér, hidden in the yard of an old apartment block. It is open only on Saturday mornings. Another unusual feature of the house of prayer at number 22 is that it follows Sephardic rites: It is sometimes called a Chortkov synagogue, referring to the Hasidic founders who arrived from the town of Czertków in what is now modern-day Ukraine.

In the first years of the 20th century, a *kloyz* (school for the religious education of adult men) was established here. At the back of the house, two ground floor apartments were joined to create the *shtiebel*, a small house of prayer. Most of the interiors are original, with a few pieces imported from other defunct prayer houses in the area. The Torah ark, the bimah, and the amud may have come from Galicia (Ukraine) – possibly gifts from the Czertków rebbe. The walls are also worth a look: They were painted using rollers, creating many different patterns.

Czertków is also the birthplace of Mayer Amschel Rothschild (1744–1812), founder of the Rothschild banking dynasty.

Jewish people were among the first settlers in this part of the city at the start of the 19th century. Most of them were of lower social status and had moved here from the countryside. A few arrived from Galicia (the Polish-Ukrainian region, not in Spain), including the founders of the Teleki tér house of prayer. Many were making their way from Galicia to America, stopping at the railway station in nearby Józsefváros, hoping to find enough work to be able to save money for their passage to America. There were also small traders and craftsmen, attracted by the local market in Teleki tér.

RELIEFS OF THE SOCIAL SECURITY CENTRE

Situations and professions covered by insurance

1081 Budapest, 19 Fiumei út
Tram: 24 – Dologház utca

Opposite the main entrance of the Fiumei út cemetery, a large office was built in two phases in the first half of the 20th century for the administration of healthcare and pension insurance. Its main facade features a series of surprising reliefs. The main hall is also well worth a look with its curved arches and early, modern design.

Reliefs on the facade show various situations and professions covered by social and accident insurance: 25 reliefs were installed under the first-floor windows. To see all of them, start by the Alföldi utca facade, walk along Fiumei út, then turn into Dologház utca.

The first 11 pieces are more allegoric, depicting human life, the caring nature of insurance, life and death, luck and bad luck. Death appears on two of them. The topics of the next 14 pieces – on the newer, northern

wing – are more concrete: Machines appear as dangerous equipment, as causes of accidents or death. Cars appear only on this newer side. The reliefs were made by many artists. In many cases, the sculptor is unknown, as there is no signature.

The northern wing, where the customer service area is located, is now accessible to the general public. The curved ceiling features Rothalit glass pieces set into the holes of a reinforced concrete net. The lighting and desks are part of the recent reconstruction.

The large office block is the last major cooperative work by architects Marcell Komor and Dezső Jakab (between 1897 and 1918, the pair worked on the design of the Palace Hotel in Rákóczi út and on the Erkel Theatre – People's Opera – in Józsefváros).

The southern wing was built in 1913, followed by the tower and the northern wing in 1931. Between 2002 and 2004, the building was completely renewed.

The lost tower of the first 'skyscraper' of the city

When it was completed in the early 1930s, the tower was several floors higher. It had 17 floors and stood 75 metres high, with prominent battlements at the top, making it the first 'skyscraper' in Budapest – clearly inspired by the contemporary skyscrapers of the US. In the 1950s, the tower housed equipment that disrupted the broadcast of Radio Free Europe. However, the material used in its construction (high alumina cement) proved to be too weak to support the weight of the complete structure. In 1969 the top five floors of the tower were pulled down.

THE KOSSUTH MAUSOLEUM

A true hidden wonder

Fiumei út cemetery
16-18 Fiumei út - 1086 Budapest,
The mausoleums are open only on special days, check website for details
en.nori.gov.hu
Cemetery: from 7:30pm until sunset (5pm in winter, 8pm in early summer)
Guided tours available, check website for details and opening hours
Tram: 24 – Dologház utca

Although the large Fiumei út cemetery is well known to everyone, few know the incredible interiors of some of its mausoleums, the most splendid being that of Lajos Kossuth with its green onyx sarcophagus and its spectacular ceiling adorned with mosaic tiles. Designed by Dezső Kölber, the marvelous ceiling is covered with 23.5-carat gold. The tiles and the stained glass windows are the work of Miksa Róth. Above the entrance is the birth year of Kossuth, and above the exit, the year of his death. Beneath the row of windows is the coat of arms of the Kossuth family. Small side chapels contain the relatives of Kossuth: his sons Ferenc Lajos and Tivadar, his daughter-in-law Mária Kvassay, his wife Terézia Meszlényi, their daughter Vilma, and Kossuth's sister Lujza. The mausoleum was restored in 2015.

Following the death of Lajos Kossuth while in exile, his funeral service on 1 April 1894 was both a political protest and an historical event. The number of pallbearers was unprecedented in the country's history, and the queue of mourners was over five kilometres long. His mausoleum, completed by 1909, is the tallest funeral building in Hungary - and also works as a lookout tower.

The competition to design the memorial was won by Kálmán Gerster and Alajos Stróbl. As a lot of mourners were expected to visit, the memorial was given a front entrance and a rear exit to allow for a continuous flow of people. The entrance is guarded by two stone leopards, with the female figure of Hungaria above them. The baldachin (stone canopy) is reminiscent of the Parthenon in Athens. On top, the statue of Liberty is removing chains from a lion, symbolising Hungary in an allegoric depiction of the 1848-1849 revolution and war of independence, in which Kossuth played a major role.

Another splendid mausoleum is that of the renowned 19th century politician, Ferenc Deák, built in 1887. Inspired by Renaissance and classic Greek art, the dome is covered with Zsolnay tiles, with an angel figure on top holding a wreath and a palm branch. The interior is clad in colourful marbles and granite. The building was completely restored in 2000-2003.

The dome of the Mihály Károlyi memorial has unique acoustics. A person speaking in one corner can be heard clearly by someone standing in the opposite corner.

THE MEMORIAL OF PRIME MINISTER JÓZSEF ANTALL

An astonishing work of art

Fiumei út cemetery
16-18 Fiumei út - 1086 Budapest,
en.nori.gov.hu
From 7:30am until sunset (5pm in winter, 8pm in early summer)
Tram: 24 – Dologház utca

Inaugurated in 1999, the memorial for József Antall (prime minister of Hungary between 1990 and 1993) is an astonishing work of art by sculptor Miklós Melocco that doesn't look like anything you have seen before: a kind of huge stone tent with four corners where we can see riding horsemen and monks praying.

The underlying idea of the memorial is to depict power instead of a portrayal of the deceased prime minister.

The memorial is built upon two axes: an East-West axis with two horsemen that symbolise secular power and a North-South axis with two monks holding a cross that symbolises ecclestial power.

At the center of everything lies the modest grave, symbol of the centre of the power.

'The monument in honour of József Antall is not a mere relic, but a reflection on the intellectual legacy of Antall as well as on the ruling power', said Melocco in an interview in 1997.

One monk, holding the cross like a weapon, looks like the actor Ádám Rajhona, while the other monk's face resembles architect Károly Kós. One of the horsemen is rather faceless (it is just falling off the horse, failing in its power). The other horseman is more glorious: Its face was modelled on that of writer Endre Gerelyes, a friend of the sculptor.

The stone used for the grave was brought from Somló Hill, where the Antall family used to own land, while the ivy was brought from the inner yard of the Semmelweiss Museum, where József Antall worked as a director in the 1980s.

SALGÓTARJÁNI STREET
JEWISH CEMETERY

An atmospheric cemetery full of artwork

1087 Budapest, 6 Salgótarjáni utca
zsidotemeto.nori.gov.hu
Sun–Thu 8am–4pm (8am–3pm in winter), Fri 8am–2pm
Tram: 37, 37A – Salgótarjáni utca, temető

Adjacent to Fiumei út Cemetery (see previous double pages), the small and almost forgotten Salgótarjáni Street Jewish Cemetery was opened in 1874. A lot of famous Hungarian Jews were buried here, many of them have tombstones that are true pieces of art, from classic to Art Nouveau and modern pieces, especially in the western part.

Due to its small size, the cemetery was almost full by the beginning of the 20th century. After the war, the cemetery was practically abandoned, as there was practically no one to tend the graves. Most of the monuments decayed and vegetation took over. Despite recent works, the cemetery still feels almost abandoned.

Along the fence behind the funeral home are some of the most exquisite monuments. The large gravestone with eagles on four sides is of the Vázsonyi family: Minister of Justice Vilmos Vázsonyi was the first Jewish Hungarian to become a minister. The nearby grave of Adolf Temesváry features a winged lion.

A large nicely restored memorial can be seen a little farther along. Its elegant colonnade and symbolic sarcophagus were built for the Weiss family: Manfréd Weiss was the founder of the Weiss Manfréd Works (later Csepel Works) industrial complex (see p. 286).

Farther on, on the other side of the narrow path is a bomb crater from the Second World War.

Head right at the crossing for the magnificent Hatvany-Deutsch family mausoleum. The family laid the foundations of Hungary's mill and sugar industry and their descendants were famous art collectors. Brewery owner Sándor Hatvany-Deutsch once said: 'One of my sons is a painter, the other is also a fool.' The fool was Lajos Hatvany, co-founder of the Nyugat literature periodical, friend of poets Endre Ady and Árpád Tóth and patron of poet Attila József. His brother Ferenc Hatvany was an impressionist artist.

The path on the left after the simpler gravestones leads to a memorial dedicated to ghetto victims.

Back towards the entrance is the black stone memorial of Sámuel Goldberger, the wealthiest man in Óbuda's textile industry. On the left near the exit are the graves of some famous personalities: The Art Nouveau gravestone of rabbi Dr. Vilmos Bacher features contoured edges and floral patterns and was the very last work of Béla Lajta in 1918. The simple flat gravestone of impressionist painter Adolf Fényes is also located here.

THE GARDEN OF COUNTIES

A forgotten witness of Budapest's unification centenary

1101 Budapest, Népliget – opposite Bíró Lajos utca
Metro: M3 – Népliget

Built within Népliget Park as part of the centenary celebrations of the unification of Pest, Buda and Óbuda, the Garden of Counties (or Centenary Park) was inaugurated on 1 October 1973. Although it is largely forgotten today, it is well worth a visit. The stroll around the various plants, rocks and artworks that each of the 19 counties of Hungary sent to the capital city at that time is a very charming way to travel back

instantly to 1973. Reeds from the Fertő lake area, grey granite from the Badacsony region, pine trees from the Mátras, etc. – everything was originally connected by a path made from railway sleepers, symbolising the national rail network.

Baranya county's gift was a roughly two-metre-high stone obelisk with curved shapes. A similar, but simpler piece of carved stone marks the name of Fejér county, with the coat of arms of the county seen above on one side, and the coat of arms of Székesfehérvár and Dunaújváros carved into the opposite side of the stone. A larger circular relief showing the county of Borsod-Abaúj-Zemplén surrounded by the coats of arms of the larger towns has survived in relatively good condition, probably because the plants around it make it harder to find. Unfortunately, the 'folk style' wooden benches nearby have all gone missing.

The county of Békés donated a small water fountain made of three stone spheres representing the 'triple Kőrös' rivers of the area. The spheres are still there, but without any water. Veszprém's section features elevated basalt stone beds for the trees, representing the hills of the Badacsony region that were once formed by volcanic activity. To represent the Göcsej region of Zala county, sculptor János Németh created a large (approximately 320 x 130 cm) ceramic wall relief: one of the two artworks in the garden that was restored. On one side there are four people (including the crucified Jesus) and two animals, while the other side depicts agricultural life in the region. Another element has been restored since 1973: The missing parts of a concrete fence donated by Tolna were replaced in 2011.

Unfortunately, several more artworks were damaged: The water fountains donated by Győr and Nógrád counties are no longer functioning and Heves' oversized pebbles are all gone.

The legacy of the celebrations of the unification of Buda, Pest and Obuda in 1973

The centenary celebrations of the unification necessitated a lot of construction, much of which remains today. The Cog-wheel Railway was renewed and new vehicles were introduced: They are still running on the line. A short text commemorating the 1973 upgrade was carved into a larger piece of rock and placed by the Városmajor terminus of the line.

Metro line M1 was extended to Mexikói út. Beforehand, the line was elevated to the surface and had its terminus by the zoo. Since 1973, it has had two new stops: Széchenyi fürdő and Mexikói út (a memorial stone sign can be seen at Széchenyi fürdő station). The Ganz factory produced new vehicles for the occasion: These unique vehicles, with rather low ceilings due to the size constraints of the tunnel, are still running on the line. Interestingly, the M1 line had a 'drive on the left' rule until 1973, even though traffic in Hungary was changed to driving on the right in 1941, in order to harmonise the rule with neighbouring countries. There is only one

line in Hungary that keeps running on the left side: the HÉV line that runs to Gödöllő.

Overpasses were built in Jászberényi út, Árpád út and in Ócsai út and the first multi-storey carpark built in Budapest since the Second World War was erected in Szervita tér by Interag (replaced today by a new office building). Attila József housing estate was also presented with a new cinema called Pest-Buda.

Chain Bridge and the Tunnel were restored: The mosaic tile cladding of the tunnel is from 1973 (there is a small memorial sign of the 1973 works by the tunnel's entrance, close to the funicular called Budavári Sikló).

The House of Soviet Science and Culture was opened in the building at the corner of Kossuth Lajos utca and Semmelweis utca (see p. 110). A large-scale exhibition was also opened about the history of Budapest, featuring a large wooden model of the central part of the city (see picture). A Budapest Encyclopedia was published, and several short films were also created about the past and present of the capital city.

NATIONAL EDUCATIONAL LIBRARY AND MUSEUM

The 'Fairy Palace' of Budapest

1087 Budapest, 40 Könyves Kálmán körút
opkm.hu
Check website for opening hours
Metro: M3 – Népliget

Nicknamed the 'Fairy Palace' due to its Art Nouveau and Art Deco detailing, the beautiful building at 40 Könyves Kálmán körút houses the plant collection of the Natural History Museum (unfortunately not open to visitors) and the National Educational Library and Museum, along with an external branch of the National Museum where restorers are trained.

The museum, therefore, is a great excuse to visit the impressive interiors, with decorations inspired by Hungarian folk patterns and late Art Nouveau, as well as the beautiful sgraffito on the facade with its geometric patterns enclosing a studying pupil.

The building was originally designed in 1911 by Albert Kálmán Kőrössy as a grammar school. It was one of the first schools to have specialised classrooms: geography, biology and physics facilities were built. Up to 500 people could fit into the main assembly hall.

Opened in 1968, the museum displays equipment used by teachers in Hungary during the last century and, as such, is the largest collection of its kind in Central and Eastern Europe. Its mission is to collect and display the material objects supporting public education. Visitors can discover how their parents and grandparents were taught, how school life was decades or centuries ago, and what demonstration tools, desks, tables and other objects were used to support education.

THE GLASS WINDOW OF SEMMELWEIS UNIVERSITY

Hungary's largest glass window

1089 Budapest,
Nagyvárad tér
Open during university hours only, closed for summer
Metro: M3 – Nagyvárad tér

Inside Semmelweis University, a huge glass window with bright colours and non-figurative patterns resembling cells under a microscope is familiar to students of the medical university, but remains unknown to most inhabitants of Budapest. With an area of 150 square metres, it is Hungary's largest glass window.

To see it, one has to enter one of the tallest buildings in the city, namely the tower of Semmelweis University in Nagyvárad tér, close to the metro station. The window is just opposite the main entrance.

The window is the result of a competition that was held to design a colourful artwork for the hall.

It was won by Gyula Hincz (1904–1986), who understood the hall's *genius loci* (spirit of place) and designed a non-figurative work inspired by the world of microbiology.

Designed in 1973, it was installed here in early 1982.

The 21 x 7-metre window is made up of large and small circles, contrasting intricacies, and abstract shapes, inspired by the world of cells and their composition, appearing almost psychedelic. Hincz called this style 'amoebism'.

The peace inscriptions

Returning to the square from the tower, a large statue dominates the corner. On top of a mound clad in grey granite bricks is a large abstract bird with outstretched wings.

Sculpted in 1983 by Péter Székely, the bird symbolises peace. Among the grey bricks is a pink marble plaque bearing the words *béke* ('peace' in Hungarian), with the signature of János Kádár, communist leader of Hungary between 1956 and 1988, and *paix* ('peace' in French), with the signature of former French president Francois Mitterrand.

Both leaders were patrons of the creation of this work, a monument to the peace process between the communist and capitalist worlds. The word 'peace' can be spotted in many other languages on other grey stone bricks. The grey granite came from Western Hungary, while the marble came from France.

31

SONNENSCHEIN HOUSE

A sign that commemorates a person who never existed

1094 Budapest, 15 Bokréta utca
Tram: 51, 51A – Bokréta utca

Although a large sign on the house at 15 Bokréta utca reads 'Emmá-nuel Sonnenschein & Tsa. Liqueur 1870', no one called Sonnen-schein has ever lived or worked here.

The house was built in 1867 for entrepreneur Ferenc Heigl, based on plans by Ferenc Wieser. The upper floor was added in the 1890s, when it was owned by Ferenc Heigl and Gertrúd Kreisz. Over the course of

the 20th century the house slowly deteriorated, and by the 1990s it was in very poor condition. Then something rather unusual happened …

In the mid-1990s, film director István Szabó and cameraman Lajos Koltai were scouting locations for their new historical drama *Sunshine*. This house was ideal: It was from the right era, had not been modernised and it overlooked the square. The film tells the fictional story of three generations of the Sonnenschein family and the liqueur production business it ran from this house: In the 19th century this area was home to many small businesses.

Not only was the sign added to the house, but the façade was decorated and the ashlar on the ground floor level was cut into smaller pieces and brick inserts were added – inspired by the look of some neighbouring houses. When the house was renovated in 2008, these decorations were preserved.

32

PSYART COLLECTION OF THE HUNGARIAN ACADEMY OF SCIENCES

Out of the ordinary artwork by out of the ordinary people

1907 Budapest, 4 Tóth Kálmán utca, Building B
psyartcoll.mta.hu/hu/kapcsolat
For a visit (in small groups), prior booking is needed
Tram: 2, 24 – Haller utca/Soroksári út

By prior arrangement, it is possible to visit the surprising art collection of the former institutes of psychiatry. Most of the artists of this unique collection were not professionals: they were the patients of the institutes. Their activity emerged spontaneously, by encouragement, or, from the 1960s, as part of their treatment. Hence the varying artistic quality of the collection's items whose value lies in giving a glimpse into troubled minds.

Dr. Árpád Selig started to collect and display the works in the 1910s. Later, he became the director of the Angyalföld Institute where most of the works were created along with the Lipótmező Institute. Following Selig's early death, Dr. István Zsakó continued to collect the works and opened a museum in 1931 in the former Angyalföld Institute before the collections of the two institutes were merged in 1936.

During the Second World War, the items were packed away and the collection was split up, but the fragmented collection was re-organised by museologists and exhibited again in 1988 in Lipótmező, until the closure of the institute in 2007. After that, the collection was handed over to the Hungarian Academy of Sciences and a small exhibition was opened in 2017 in its current location.

Most of the current collection originates from the 1920s–1940s and the 1970s–1980s. The largest artwork is a model of the Lipótmező building complex from the second half of the 1910s. Some pieces of art are more traditional: clay models, small sculptures, paintings, drawings etc. Some works are from artists like János Bártfai, a little-known painter who focused his ink drawings and paintings on his 'travels to Mars', or from the infamous serial killer Marinko Magda, whose most well-known crime was the killing of the Z. Nagy family in Szeged in 1994. His dreadful drawings are part of the collection today (thanks to a purchase by András Veér), while the criminal is serving his sentence in prison.

Unfortunately, there are no works by Lajos Gulácsy, a master of early 20th-century Hungarian painting, who became a patient of the institute in 1917 due to severe schizophrenia.

K&H BANK CUSTOMER SERVICE AREA

33

The set of a sci-fi film?

South atrium
1095 Budapest, 9 Lechner Ödön fasor
Mon–Thu 8am–4:30pm, Friday 8am–3pm
Tram: 2, 24 – Müpa – Nemzeti Színház; Bus: 23, 54, 55 – Müpa – Nemzeti
Színház; HÉV: H7 – Müpa – Nemzeti Színház

Few people, apart from the bank's customers, usually enter the head-quarters of K&H Bank, opened in 2011, but people are really missing something. For a truly extraordinary experience, head to the south atrium (open to the general public) and the customer service area there: Designed by Finta Studio, its futuristic interior really looks like the set of a sci-fi film.

Illuminated by large 'UFOs' suspended from the ceiling, the space is divided up by organic mushroom-like columns, with the aim of providing a cool and unique experience for visitors, light-years away from the traditional image of banking.

As banking has moved increasingly online, local branches have functioned more like meeting places, somewhere to conduct personal business rather than just financial transactions. There is no counter here between employee and customer: The glossy toroid-shaped seating encourages a more direct, informal means of communication.

THE ENGINE ROOM OF THE FERENCVÁROS PUMP STATION

34

Century-old equipment still in working order

1095 Budapest, 31 Soroksári út
Group tours only
Email for bookings: center@fcsm.hu
Tram: 1, 2, 24 – Közvágóhíd

One of the sewage and rainwater pump stations of the Budapest Sewage Works offers visitors an unexpected glimpse into history: The century-old equipment it houses is still in working order.

Construction of the sewage network on the Pest side, between Jászai Mari tér and Boráros tér, began at the end of the 19th century, both along the ring road and along the Danube. Water was collected in large pipes connected to a sewage treatment site built close to the river.

When the site began operating in 1893, steam engines were used to pass water through a two-section mud chamber, before it was ejected into the Danube by six pairs of pumps. One steam engine operated two pumps, and five boilers were needed to create steam for the engines.

On the orders of the mayor, the pump station was converted from steam to electric power in several phases between 1924 and 1931. A transformer was put in, the mud chamber was rebuilt, and two new filter grids were added. Diesel engines were also installed to provide electricity in case of a blackout. One of these (installed in 1932) is still fully functional. If there is a serious flood, 'Grandma' can be used: This engine was brought here at the turn of the century by a navy vessel, and can offset the pressure of up to eight metres of water in the Danube. The site was heavily bombed during the Second World War, but was then reconstructed by 1947. Another major reconstruction began in 1971, preserving the old engine room. Today, waste water is pumped from here to a treatment site in Csepel.

A decade after the construction of the site in Ferencváros, a second site was built in Zsigmond tér. That building cannot be visited, but is worth a look from the outside. Also of interest is the nearby waterworks site in Árpád fejedelem útja, located between the HÉV rail tracks and the Danube.

The memento of a dark period of Hungarian history in an air raid shelter

1097 Budapest, Fék utca 6
Visited only in groups of 5 to 40 people, with prior booking at
malenkij@mnm.hu
For more information: 307 015 223
Tram: 1 – Ferencváros vasútállomás – Málenkij Robot Emlékhely; MÁV train:
Ferencváros

Right by Ferencváros railway station, a large concrete slab is decorated with metal 'sculptures' of train carriages cut in half. They were placed there in memory of a tragic chapter of Hungarian history: the suffering of those taken to forced labour camps by the Soviets. The large concrete block houses an exhibition about this period, and can be viewed with prior booking only.

The exhibition tells the story of one of Hungary's darkest periods: the 'malenki robot', as it was called in Russian. Although it has to be booked in advance, the visit is well worth the effort: It recounts a less well-known chapter of the Second World War in a truly unique location, with a lot of information and a few original objects.

The windowless block was built after the Second World War as an air raid shelter and leadership coordination point of the Hungarian State

Railways. At the end of the war, the occupying Red Army defeated the German troops, and the following ceasefire agreement secured the way for the exploitation of the locals: they were taken away by the thousands for 'malenkaia rabota', i.e. 'small work' (the sarcastic term referring to forced labour), to serve in one of the labour camps of the 'Gupvi' in the Soviet Union (Gupvi was the system of forced labour camps under Stalin's rule).

Upon entering, visitors can learn about the Second World War siege of the city. The next section tells of the deportation of civilians, illustrated with objects that depict life (and death) in the labour camps: clothes, wooden cases etc. Another section details the grim fate of Carpathian Ruthenians – their oppression and destruction was part of Stalin's plan to annex Ruthenia to the Soviet Empire. Those who didn't die on the long walk had a good chance of catching epidemic typhus or dying from famine.

The next section describes the roughly 350 camps and almost 4,000 sub-camps that at their peak reached 7 million prisoners. It is estimated that the total number of Hungarians taken there reached 1 million people: The exact number remains unclear due to lack of records. As you can see on the museum maps, the majority of them worked in today's Eastern Ukraine area, mostly in the coal mines – hence the coal wagon on the main façade of this memorial place.

The other part of this section details the miserable life in the crowded barracks, surrounded by barbed wire fences. The last section tells of the return of the survivors, starting from 1946, and the commemoration. Those who returned were forced into silence for decades. Only the fall of Communism changed that. The Compensation Law of 1992 granted compensation to the few remaining survivors.

THE BUNKERS
OF THE CSEPEL WORKS

(36)

A glimpse into the hardships of the Second World War

1211 Budapest, Színesfém utca
budapestscenes.com
Guided tours only (see website)
HÉV: H7 – Szent Imre tér; Bus: 38, 38A, 138, 179, 238, 278 – Szent Imre tér

A 250-hectare plot in the heart of the Isle of Csepel was once home to the Csepel Works (formerly Manfréd Weiss Steel and Metal Works plc), a large industrial complex supplemented by a network of bunkers. As a supplier to the army, it was a target in the Second World War and the workers needed protection: Up to 25,000 used the main gate during the conflict.

Between 1938 and 1944, more than 150 air raid shelters were built, including 17 particularly strong ones built in 1943–44 designed to resist bombs, gas attacks and shrapnel. And they worked: The survival rate of the factory workers was much higher than that of the other citizens of Budapest – the city that endured the second largest siege of any city in the war. At the end of the Socialist Era, much of the old equipment vanished from the bunkers, one of which was turned into a visitor attraction.

One of the most noticeable aspects of these facilities is that they are not subterranean. There are two reasons for this: one is that due to the nearby Danube, the groundwater level is high; the other is that digging deep would have required a lot of time and money. Increasing the thickness of the reinforced concrete walls proved to be the quicker option, a vital factor in wartime. The walls are so thick that they occupy almost half of the gross area in bunker two.

The first section of the bunker included showers and an air pressure adjustment system: Higher internal pressure prevented the influx of poisonous gases. Furniture is very sparse, as workers were meant to stay inside for no more than 6–8 hours.

Visitors can view short films about the memories of survivors, and are welcome to check out some of the relics on show, including gas masks, leaflets that were distributed to US soldiers, and a working air defence siren.

SOUTH-PEST WASTEWATER TREATMENT PLANT

37

A greenhouse that is part of the city's wastewater treatment

1238 Budapest, 1 Meddőhányó utca
fcsm.hu
Open during events around World Water Day, 22 March – see website
Also open for group visits: center@fcsm.hu
HÉV: H6 – Torontál utca; Bus: 66, 66B, 166 – Torontál utca

There are three large sites in Budapest for the treatment of wastewater: one in North-Pest, one in Csepel and one in South-Pest. The latter one was planned in 1952, came into operation in 1966, and has been modernised in several steps since 1997 to incorporate the latest treatment technologies.

A visit offers three key opportunities: Understand how a water treatment plant functions, discover the history of Budapest's wastewater treatment and admire the large greenhouse that is part of the cleaning process and is the most beautiful part of the site. Plants in the greenhouse take part in filtering the water, a process that produces biogas that can be used to produce heating and electricity, making the site almost completely self-sufficient.

As visitors go by on the walkway (metal grids), water is flowing below their feet, while large palm trees and bamboo create a truly green environment under the glass roofing. Even butterflies have been brought into the process: They prevent the overpopulation of ladybirds and other insects that would harm the plants. The butterflies also help to pollinate the flowering plants.

Surrounding the greenhouses, large circular basins were built to collect rainwater. Their capacity was increased in 2019 as part of preparations for climate change, due to a higher chance of rapid rainfalls that fill up the network of pipes quickly, inundating the water treatment site.

Annually, approximately 22 million cubic metres of wastewater is treated here with a better quality of water flowing into the Danube than the EU directives demand. The rainwater and wastewater are collected from the region through a network of pipes that are more than 6,000 kilometres in length.

ANTAL NEMCSICS MEMORIAL HOUSE

38

Immerse yourself in the world of colours

Country of colours gallery
1185 Budapest, 42 Ungvár utca
Wed 9am–3pm, Sat 2pm–6pm, or by prior registration for groups at nemcsics.
csongor@t-online.hu
MÁV trains: Ferihegy; Tram: 50 – Bajcsy-Zsilinszky út

O n the outskirts of Budapest, the Antal Nemcsics Memorial House is a beautiful tribute to a really extraordinary man. A painter, university teacher and master of colours, all at the same time, Antal Nemcsics (1927–2019) even developed a new colour system, the Coloroid system (see below).

Opened in 2020, the memorial is the former house of Antal Nemcsics and his wife, Magdona Takács, who was also a painter.

The most interesting part is the very atmospheric 6-metre-high studio, used during their lifetime, that functions today as a gallery for their works, which are mostly colourful paintings.

Two further rooms in the house are used for temporary exhibitions for Hungarian artists.

Antal Nemcsics and the Coloroid system

A very active artist, Antal Nemcsics (1927–2019) created paintings, frescoes, stained glass, mosaics and ceramic artworks. More than a hundred churches have murals painted by him. He wrote 24 books and more than 300 publications, made 11 inventions, created colouring plans for public buildings as well as for the 13th district of Budapest, and created a colour scheme for line 3 of the Metro in the early 1990s, during the extension of the line.

The colour coding system that he proposed and that appeared in the new stations (from Forgách utca to Újpest-Központ) was unfortunately completely destroyed during the latest renovation of the line, but two of his works survived: a yellow-black-white enamel mural in Forgách utca metro station, titled Surface and Depth – an abstract description of descending from the sunlight of the surface to the 'darkness' of the metro station. A similar work, showing a transition from dark blue to white can be seen in the Gyöngyösi utca metro station. He also took part in the colouring of the old houses of the Castle District to create a harmonious view along the historic streets. One of his murals, depicting horsemen in an abstract form, can be seen there on the side of a house in Nőegylet utca.

During the 1970s, he developed a new colour system, called Coloroid. This system was revolutionary in its ability to give a scientific, numeric description to the harmony of colours, beyond subjective impressions. The system was published in multiple countries like Argentina, the United States, Canada and Japan. His textbook on colour dynamics was published in London, Zurich, Budapest, Göttingen, New York, Tokyo, Toronto, Sydney and Singapore.

MERZSE SWAMP

One of the last remaining accessible swamps in Budapest

1174 Budapest, Erdőalatti dűlő
MÁV – Rákoskert; Bus 197 – Rákoskert vasútállomás
Full walk: 6 kilometres

To the north of Liszt Ferenc International Airport is one of the last remaining accessible swamps in Budapest. Home to protected plants and many rare and protected birds, it is a great place to escape the city and spend a few hours in a beautiful and uncrowded natural setting, close to the city centre.

From the end of the station platform at Rákoskert, a dirt track leads to Merzse parking lot.

Displayed here (in Hungarian only) is a table containing information about the area. A narrow path with green frog signs marks the way, and soon the swamp will appear on the right. There are a few old trees which can be climbed, before following the path round to the right and reaching the lookout tower, which is the best place from which to view the area.

The swamp area gained protected status in 1977, and was later extended in 1999 to a total of 40 acres. In 2012 the path and information tables were created. From tables 8 and 9 there is a shortcut around the expanse of water, and further on is Gyolcs field. The full walk is about six kilometres (cycling is also permitted).

The water is surrounded by dense reeds and sedge, interspersed with willow and cottonwood trees, the latter planted for forestry. Binoculars or a strong zoom lens are recommended.

RENÉE ERDŐS HOUSE

One of the most beautiful villas of the 17th district

1174 Budapest, 31 Báthory utca
erdosreneehaz.hu
Tue–Sun 2pm–6pm
Bus: 198 – Bánya part or 46, 98 – Bulyovszky utca; MÁV – Rákoshegy

Built in 1895, the Renée Erdős House at 31 Báthori utca is one of the most beautiful villas of the 17th district. In 1927 Renée Erdős, a well-known writer of the era, purchased the house and lived there until 1944. Since 1990 it has been home to a local history collection.

To the left of the entrance, along with a few palaeontological finds (such as mammoth bones and fossilised pieces of wood), a diorama depicts the wildlife of the Merzse swamp nature reserve (see p. 292) across all four seasons. The central room features descriptions of the four small towns which make up the district today: Rákoshegy, Rákosliget, Rákoscsaba and Rákoskeresztúr.

Left again and the demographic history of the area is on show, including traditional clothing worn in Slovakian and German communities, an old wooden chariot, and parts of interiors from old farmhouses. To the right, a small shop offers literature and postcards.

On the upper level are temporary exhibitions, along with a small room dedicated to the memory of Renée Erdős. The furniture in here is from the era, although the only pieces originally owned by the writer are the two copper bed ends.

Renée Erdős

Renée Erdős (1879–1956) was a contentious writer and poet. Her passion and uncompromising honesty left no one untouched. She had relationships with several famous personalities of the era, including Sándor Bródy and Oszkár Jászi. Following Bródy's suicide attempt in 1905, Erdős was considered a femme fatale. She lived a turbulent life: Her work was often rejected by publishers, her first marriage failed, she was forced to hide during the Second World War, and her writing was banned in the communist era because it included erotica and religious motifs, thus unacceptable to the state ideology. Most of her works were published again only after 1990.

THE SCHMIDL MAUSOLEUM

A true masterpiece of funeral architecture

Budapest Jewish Cemetery
1108 Budapest, 6 Kozma utca
budapestjewishcemetery.com
Apr–Oct 8am–4pm, Nov–Mar 8am–3pm
Tram: 28 – Izraelita temető; Bus: 68, 195 – Izraelita temető

Next to the Új Köztemető (New Public Cemetery), on the outskirts of Pest, the Budapest Jewish Cemetery was opened in 1893. Although it lies far from the city centre, it more than deserves a visit for the several architectural masterpieces that can be found there.

Not far away from the entrance and the funeral home building (designed in the arabesque style by Vilmos Freund, who also designed the cemetery itself), is the spectacular bright turquoise Schmidl mausoleum. Built in 1903 by Béla Lajta, it is probably the most beautiful piece in the cemetery.

Miklós Schmidl ordered its construction for his mother Róza Holländer and his father Sándor Schmidl, a colonial goods tradesman. The barrel-vault concrete structure is clad in magnificent Art Nouveau ceramics from the Zsolnay factory, added one year after construction. The decorative mosaics of the interior walls and ceiling were produced by Miksa Róth. The furnaces of the Alföld region give the vault its shape, while the heart-shaped leaf ornamentations are based on traditional Hungarian decorations.

In the centre of the façade, a cast-iron gate decorated with willow branches is flanked by ornamental vases and poppy heads (symbolising a long sleep). Above the gate, a flower with six petals references the Star of David. The memorial was restored in 1996–98.

THE GRAVE
OF LÁSZLÓ HARTMANN

A stone racing car on top of a grave

Budapest Jewish Cemetery
1108 Budapest, 6 Kozma utca
budapestjewishcemetery.com
Apr–Oct 8am–4pm, Nov–Mar 8am–3pm
Tram: 28 – Izraelita temető; Bus: 68, 195 – Izraelita temető

Within the Budapest Jewish Cemetery, the grave of László Hart-mann (1901–1938) is particularly original: It is topped by a beautiful stone racing car. Hartmann first started driving cars profes-sionally as a tour driver, but the real change came in his life after pur-

chasing Earl Zichy's Bugatti racing car and setting a new speed record with it. He is remembered as a champion in Grand Prix car racing – a predecessor of the current Formula 1. He raced mostly with Bugatti and Maserati cars, and died following a fatal accident during a race in 1938, competing with the Italian Guiseppe Farina. Hartmann's grave was beautifully restored in 2018.

Most of the splendid graves and crypts of rich families, some of them in quite poor condition, can be found along the Kozma utca fence, on both sides of the funeral home building. Right after the entrance is the crypt of the Brüll family, built in the shape of an antique shrine, featuring detailed mosaic decorations and two stone lions sculpted by Alajos Stróbl. Also worth visiting are the Gries crypt, the oval-shaped Weingruber grave, and the black and gold mausoleum of the Wellisch family. Famous personalities resting here include music publisher Gyula Rózsavölgyi, actor Béla Salamon, cabaret entertainer Dezső Kellér, architects Béla Lajta and Alfréd Hajós, and actor and comedian Gyula Gózon.

The cemetery also contains examples of numerous symbols which are specific to the Jewish community. More information can be found on the following double page.

Symbols on Jewish tombstones

Symbols have always played a fundamental role in Judaism. Each graphic sign is assigned a characteristic or quality and is intended to represent the link between humankind and God (unlike diabolism, which separates humankind from God) and to identify a family or a religious function.

Tombstones in Jewish cemeteries feature some common themes, notably the "priestly blessing", indicating the deceased person's priestly descent. It can be found on the tombstones of members of the Cohen (or Coen) family; in Hebrew *kohèn* means priest, i.e. a male descendent of Aaron, brother of Moses and first high priest of the Jewish community. The position of the hands, with spread fingers, is adopted during the blessing.

Another typical symbol is the pitcher pouring water. This symbol is a sign of belonging to the Israelite tribe of Levi (the Levi family), whose traditional duties were to assist priests during religious services by washing their hands before the blessing.

The oldest tombstones also bear another symbol prominent in Jewish funerary symbolism: the crown. This represents both the political authority and the dignitary role of the deceased and comes from a quote from *Pirkei Avot* (Ethics of Our Fathers), one of the founding texts of Judaism: "There are three crowns: the crown of Torah, the crown of priesthood and the crown of monarchy – but the crown of a good name outweighs them all."

From the 19th century, other symbols more in line with the trends of the time began to appear. The clepsydra refers to the

passage of time and the moment when life comes to an end. It sometimes bears wings, or can be associated with crossbones and a skull, making the connection to death even more evident. Similarly, the symbol of a torch turned upside down is used to represent mourning: The flame must be extinguished against the floor.

The ouroboros, the symbol of a serpent eating its own tail, recalls the notion of rebirth, while the crown of flowers can evoke the idea that the deceased acquired a reputation during his terrestrial life.

The butterfly, a symbol both ancient and common, refers to the soul departing the body and ascending into the sky.

The Star of David (*Magen David*) is perhaps the most famous symbol in Jewish culture. It was widely adopted throughout the 19th century and can be seen on many tombstones in cemeteries across the world.

Animal figures symbolise the name of the deceased: The lion, often seen next to a crown, not only indicates that the person is of royal descent and therefore belongs to David's lineage, it also refers to the name Leon (*Leo* in Italian, *Loeb* or *Loew* in Germany); the wolf is the emblem of Benjamin and is the representation of a very common surname in the Jewish community (*Wolf* in English and German, *Zeev* in Hebrew); and a deer, which represents descendants of the Naphtali tribe, refers to the surname *Hirsch* (in Yiddish and German), *Zvi* (in Hebrew) or *Naftali*.

NAPLÁS LAKE

A haven for wildlife since the 1970s

Naplás út, 16th district
Open year-round
HÉV: H8 or H9 – Mátyásföld repülőtér then Bus 46 to Erdei bekötőút

When the large parks of Budapest become crowded on a summer weekend, the area around Naplás Lake, in the 16th district, offers a beautiful and much quieter alternative in a protected natural habitat.

Naplás lake is a natural reserve just 15 minutes' walk from the closest bus stop. The path around the lake is also accessible by bicycle and there is a car park nearby.

The lake attracts a lot of birds (although increasing traffic deters many) and is now home to such species as the common buzzard, common kestrel, greylag goose, mallards and the European greenfinch. From a distance, the surrounding forest may seem to be dominated by locust trees, but there are more willow trees at the lakeside. Sedges and ferns also thrive in the constant humidity of the shore. The European pond turtle – the only turtle species with a natural habitat in Hungary – can also be found at the lake, identifiable by the yellow spots on its black shell.

Adjacent to the lake there are two more natural areas: the Cinkota Forest (*Cinkotai parkerdő*) and the swamp areas of Szilas Stream. The best time to see the wildlife is in the early morning when the area is less busy.

BEER DELIVERY HORSES STATUE ㊹

A cute reminder of old times

1105 Budapest, 3 Dreher Antal út
Tram 28, 37 - Sörgyár

At the end of the fence of the beer factory, a tiny statue can be spotted on a curved shaped stone pedestal. It is one of the mini statues of Mihály Kolodko (see p. 28), and reminds us of old times, when the beer produced here was distributed by horse-pulled carriages.

Another mini statue can be seen inside the area of the factory, depicting the famous old owner of the factory, Antal Dreher. That piece of art can be seen during the guided tours of the factory.

THE TOWER OF THE KEEPER

The last witness of the Kőbánya vineyards

1104 Budapest, 31 Harmat ut
facebook.com/csosztoronykert
Wed–Sun, 12noon–10pm
Bus: 85, 185 – Csősztorony

In the Kőbánya-Óhegy area of the 10th district, not far from the Kőbánya water reservoir (see following double page), the narrow tower on the unassuming building of 31 Harmat utca is not there by chance or simply to reflect the taste of its owner.

Strange as it may now seem, wine production once flourished in this area, and at a time when theft was widespread, the Magistrate of Pest decided to construct this tower in 1843 in order to keep watch over the surroundings and tackle the increasing threat of theft. The building comprises a small apartment (the home of the keeper) and the narrow watchtower, from where the whole area was visible.

It was constructed by Ferenc Brein in 1844 in a Romantic style with Gothic elements. A small 'neck' section connects the two-level apartment to a second block, from which the tower rises, along with its external spiral staircase. Over time, it has become a symbol of Kőbánya: It has even appeared on the district's coat of arms since 2000. After a devastating infestation of phylloxera (a destructive grape-eating aphid), the vineyards disappeared, and the tower became redundant: The area was built up and in 1896 the police took over the building. The building was later converted first into a pub and then a restaurant, which it remains today.

© Kőbányai Önkormányzat, Public domain, via Wikimedia Commons

KŐBÁNYA WATER RESERVOIR

A spectacular 19th-century underground reservoir

1105 Budapest, 29 Ihász utca
Open only during European Heritage Days, third weekend of September
Bus: 85, 185 – Ihász utca / Csősztorony

On the outskirts of Kőbánya, the Kőbánya Water Reservoir is a spectacular historic water reservoir opened in 1871 that can be visited once a year, during the European Heritage Days (third weekend of September), which correspond to the maintenance period of the reservoir.

The immediate impression is that of an underground cathedral: Each of the two giant basins can hold up to 11,000 cubic metres (11 tonnes) of water. They are usually filled to a depth of about six and a half metres: You can see the line of this level on the brick walls. The dark colouring is caused by the iron content of the water. Water resistance is provided by a layer of clay, which works surprisingly well, even after a century and a half. In the 1970s, four more concrete basins were added to the site, each with a capacity of 4,000 cubic metres.

Budapest is often thought of as a contrast between hilly Buda and the flatter Pest side, but the heart of the 10th district sits surprisingly high above sea level. And it's the height of this particular area, higher than Gellért Hill, that led to the construction of this water reservoir between 1869 and 1871. The original plans for the reservoir were lost long ago, but it is believed that the basins were built by Italian bricklayers.

THE CELLAR SYSTEM
OF KŐBÁNYA

47

A breathtaking underground network

1015 Budapest, 1 Előd utca / 35-37 Bánya utca
dreherzrt.hu/jelentkezes-sorturara; budapestscenes.com/kobanyai-pincetura/
sortura@asahibeer.hu
Guided tours only (see websites)
Tram: 3, 28A, 62A – Szent László tér; Bus: 9 – Liget tér

The mining of limestone began in the Kőbánya ('stone mine') district in the Middle Ages, becoming particularly intensive after the devastating flood damage of 1838 (see p. 106). This intensive excavation of limestone for construction works created a breathtaking network of underground cellars and corridors that it is now possible to visit on guided tours (see above).

Stones mined in Kőbánya were extensively used for reconstruction: Margit bridge, Matthias church, Fishermen's Bastion, the Citadel, the Opera House, the University Library (see p. 62), the Hungarian Academy of Sciences and several palaces on Andrássy út. The stones were transported on horse-drawn carriages, leaving bright coloured dust on the road, which may be the origin of the name of nearby Fehér út ('White Road'). Mining ended in 1890, leaving behind more than 32 kilometres of tunnels and a total underground area of 180,000 square metres.

First to take advantage of the available underground space were wine producers: Temperature fluctuation is less than one degree here, which is perfect for wine storage. From the mid 19th century, vineyards were complemented by the production of beer. Antal Dreher set up his brewery here in 1862, fully utilising the cellars, not only for storage, but also for clean water. Dreher grew to be the largest brewery in the country in the following decades.

During the Second World War, a secret facility was set up underground to produce engines for Messerschmidt aeroplanes, though no actual planes were assembled there. After the war, the brewery was nationalised and then privatised after 1990. Today it operates on a smaller scale, meaning it uses less water, hence the rising levels in the mines. Some of the underwater sections are now used by divers for training.

A great time to visit the cellars is during the running competition organised by BBU (bbu.hu), the Underworld Bicycle Race and St László Days, organised by the local municipality in June. Dreher also has a Brewery Museum (7-11 Jászberényi út) that offers guided tours for adults (see website above). Budapest Scenes also offers guided tours to the site.

THE SECRET JAPANESE GARDEN OF MÁRTON VARGA TECHNICAL SCHOOL AND COLLEGE

48

The oldest Japanese garden in Hungary

1149 Budapest, 56-60 Mogyoródi út
Summer: (1 April–31 Oct): Mon–Sun 8am–8pm
Winter: Mon–Sun 10am–4pm
Guided tours can be booked for groups: titkarsag.vmszki@gmail.com
Special programmes are organised in April (cherry blossom), in September
(European Heritage Days) and in June (the Night of Museums)
Tram: 3, 62, 62A – Jeszenák János utca

Hidden in the backyard of the gardening and geodesy school named after Márton Varga, behind the greenhouses, the Japanese garden is a real beauty. It takes its name from some of the plants that were donated by a Japanese prince. Much less famous than the Japanese garden of Margitsziget (Margaret Island), this secret gem is a much better place to find tranquillity.

Designed by Márton Varga, the founder of the school, the garden was first opened in 1928 and was the first Japanese garden in Hungary. In 1931 prince Nobuhito Takamatsu and his wife paid a short visit to the Japanese garden and donated plants from Japan after they returned home. A few of these are still in the garden, such as an orixa japonica bush, a Chinese wisteria, an acer ginnala tree and a Hibiscus syriacus. The stones in the garden are limestone rock, brought here on horse-drawn carriages from Svábhegy, when the cog-wheel railway was under reconstruction.

The garden suffered damage in the Second World War, but was renewed and extended during the following decades. Today, it occupies about 3,000 square metres. A small wooden structure, an *azumaya*, is used as a tea house. Although the oldest and largest tree is a Norway maple, the most interesting tree is probably the dawn redwood, once declared extinct until its rediscovery in 1944 in China. Hungary was able to obtain some seeds which were propagated here, and today a 28-metre-high tree stands in this very garden. It is at its most beautiful in early autumn, when its leaves turn rust brown. The garden also boasts a gingko biloba and, of course, a flowering cherry tree: The current one is a 'child' of the tree that was donated by Prince Takamatsu.

Other Japanese gardens in Budapest can be found in the Füvészkert, on Margaret Island and in the zoo.

ALPHABETICAL INDEX

NOTES

NOTES

Thomas Jonglez

It was September 1995 and Thomas Jonglez was in Peshawar, the northern Pakistani city 20 kilometres from the tribal zone he was to visit a few days later. It occurred to him that he should record the hidden aspects of his native city, Paris, which he knew so well. During his seven-month trip back home from Beijing, the countries he crossed took in Tibet (entering clandestinely, hidden under blankets in an overnight bus), Iran and Kurdistan. He never took a plane but travelled by boat, train or bus, hitchhiking, cycling, on horseback or on foot, reaching Paris just in time to celebrate Christmas with the family.

On his return, he spent two fantastic years wandering the streets of the capital to gather material for his first 'secret guide', written with a friend. For the next seven years he worked in the steel industry until the passion for discovery overtook him. He launched Jonglez Publishing in 2003 and moved to Venice three years later.

In 2013, in search of new adventures, the family left Venice and spent six months travelling to Brazil, via North Korea, Micronesia, the Solomon Islands, Easter Island, Peru and Bolivia. After seven years in Rio de Janeiro, he now lives in Berlin with his wife and three children.

Jonglez Publishing produces a range of titles in nine languages, released in 40 countries.

FROM THE SAME PUBLISHER

ATLAS

Atlas of extreme weathers
Atlas of geographical curiosities
Atlas of unusual wines

PHOTO BOOKS

Abandoned America
Abandoned Asylums
Abandoned Australia
Abandoned Belgium
Abandoned Churches: Unclaimed places
  of worship
Abandoned cinemas of the world
Abandoned France
Abandoned Germany
Abandoned Italy
Abandoned Japan
Abandoned Lebanon
Abandoned Spain
Abandoned USSR
After the Final Curtain – The Fall of the American
  Movie Theater
After the Final Curtain – America's Abandoned
  Theaters
Baikonur – Vestiges of the Soviet space programme
Cinemas – A French heritage
Destination Wellness – The 35 best places
  in the world to take time out
Forbidden France
Forbidden Places – Vol. 1
Forbidden Places – Vol. 2
Forbidden Places – Vol. 3
Forgotten Heritage
Oblivion
Secret sacred sites
Venice deserted
Venice from the skies

'SOUL OF' GUIDES

Soul of Amsterdam
Soul of Athens
Soul of Barcelona
Soul of Berlin
Soul of Kyoto
Soul of Lisbon
Soul of Los Angeles
Soul of Marrakesh
Soul of New York
Soul of Rome
Soul of Tokyo
Soul of Venice

'SECRET' GUIDES

Secret Amsterdam
Secret Bali – An unusual guide
Secret Bangkok
Secret Barcelona
Secret Bath – An unusual guide
Secret Belfast
Secret Berlin
Secret Brighton – An unusual guide
Secret Brooklyn
Secret Brussels
Secret Buenos Aires
Secret Campania
Secret Cape Town
Secret Copenhagen
Secret Corsica
Secret Dolomites
Secret Dublin – An unusual guide
Secret Edinburgh – An unusual guide
Secret Florence
Secret French Riviera
Secret Geneva
Secret Glasgow
Secret Granada
Secret Helsinki
Secret Istanbul
Secret Johannesburg
Secret Lisbon
Secret Liverpool – An unusual guide
Secret London – An unusual guide
Secret London – Unusual bars & restaurants
Secret Los Angeles
Secret Madrid
Secret Mexico City
Secret Milan
Secret Montreal – An unusual guide
Secret Naples
Secret New Orleans
Secret New York – An unusual guide
Secret New York – Curious activities
Secret New York – Hidden bars & restaurants
Secret Paris
Secret Prague
Secret Provence
Secret Rio
Secret Rome
Secret Seville
Secret Singapore
Secret Sussex – An unusual guide
Secret Tokyo
Secret Tuscany
Secret Venice
Secret Vienna
Secret Washington D.C.

Follow us on Facebook, Instagram and X

ACKNOWLEDGEMENTS

Nagy Zita, Dr. Péter Fodor, Zsuzsanna Juhász (Metropolitan Ervin Szabó Library / Budapest Collection; Orsolya Eleőd (Hotel Hilton); The Communications Department of BKV Zrt.; Pataki Márk (Pinball Museum); Márton Kovács, Bálint György (Communications Department of the Parliament); Judit Villám (Library of the Hungarian Parliament); Levente Péter (Cinema History Collection); Tóth János Csaba (St Stephen's Basilica); Anett Nagy (Festetics Palace / Andrássy University); Géza Balázs Popovics, Bernadett Szentmiklósi (Károli Gáspár Reformed University); Zsófia Kancler (Museum of Applied Arts); Ágnes Anna Sebestyén (Museum of Hungarian Architecture); Ildikó Balogh (ELTE University Library and Archives); János László (Civertan Studio – legifoto.com); Norbert Keserű (Budapest City Archives); Diós István (Seminarium Centrale); Attila Jeney (2 Papnövelde utca); Flóra Bartók, Emese Zsoldos, Márta Branczik, Balázs Maczó, Loránd Balla (Budapest History Museum / Kiscelli Museum); Fanni Fodor (Imre Nagy Foundation); Gábor Kampis (Imre Makovecz Foundation); Dr. Áron Keve Kiss (Svábhegy Observatory); Árpád Bálint (Törley Museum); Dr. Antal Sásdi (Péterfy Sándor utca Hospital and Health Centre); Piroska Martsa (Martsa Studios); Judit Faludy (PsyArt Collection of the HAS); Marianna Bátori (Budapest Sewage Works Pte Ltd.); Levente Somogyi, Péter Horváth (Budapest Scenes); Csongor Nemcsics (Antal Nemcsics Memorial House); Julie & Victor Forrester

PHOTOGRAPHY CREDITS

Photos were taken by the author, with the following exceptions:
Fortepan / Friss Ildikó: Frescoes of the National Archives
Fortepan / Kádas Tibor: József Gruber water reservoir
Fortepan / Weygand Tibor: The plaque of the former hydroplane station
Fortepan / Somlai Tibor: The library of the Technical University
Courtesy of the Parliament Library, photo: Roberto Nencini: The Parliament library
Courtesy of the Parliament Libaray, photo: Judit Villam: The Parliament library
Attila Terbócs and Lo Scaligero: Photos of Beviacqua Palace
egykor.hu: The forgotten metallic structure of the former National Casino
Museum of Applied Arts / Muveszi Ipar, 1892: Károlyi-Csekonics Palace
Budapest City Archives, BFL XV.16.b.221/cop11: Remains of the old city wall, map
Jakab Warschag / Wikipedia Commons : Remains of the old city wall, old drawing
Fortepan / Somlai Tibor: Library of the central seminary
ELTE University Library and Archives, Budapest: University library of ELTE
Fortepan / BFL / Klösz György: University library of ELTE
ELTE University Library and Archives, Budapest: University library of ELTE
Fortepan / Stipkovits Fülöp: Former silk manufacture in Óbuda
Fortepan / Lőrinczi Ákos: Napraforgó Utca Estate
Fortepan / Nagy Józsefné dr : The Svábhegy Observatory
Fortepan / BFL / Klösz György: Széchenyi gloriette
Fortepan / Gárdos György: The church of Külső Kelenföld parish
Photo Courtesy of FKF: Municipal waste recycling facility
Wikimedia Commons: Statue of the warrior of the Hungarian Red Army
zsoltbatr: The staircase of the Kozmo Hotel
Metropolitan Ervin Szabó Library Budapest Collection: Reliefs of the social security centre
Fortepan / Fortepan: The garden of the counties
Fortepan / Építésügyi Dokumentációs és Információs Központ: The garden of the counties
Courtesy of K&H Bank: K&H Bank Customer Service Area
Civertan.hu: South Pest water treatment plant

Maps: : **Cyrille Suss** – Layout: **Emmanuelle Willard Toulemonde** – Copy-editing: **Sigrid Newman and Lee Dickinson** – Proofreading: **Abigail Kafka** – Publishing: **Clémence Mathé**

In accordance with jurisprudence (Toulouse 14-01-1887), the publisher is not to be held responsible for any involuntary errors or omissions that may appear in the guide despite the care taken by the editorial staff. Any reproduction of this book in any format is prohibited without the express agreement of the publisher.

© JONGLEZ 2024
Registration of copyright: June 2024 – Edition: 01
ISBN: 978-2-36195-445-1
Printed in Bulgaria by Dedrax